THE WHOLE MAN

THE WHOLE MAN

EVOLVING MASCULINITY

CHRISTOPHER VEAL

NEW DEGREE PRESS

COPYRIGHT © 2022 CHRISTOPHER VEAL

THE WHOLE MAN:

Evolving Masculinity

ISBN   979-8-88504-068-6 *Paperback*

          979-8-88504-624-4 *Kindle Ebook*

          979-8-88504-174-4 *Ebook*

Tayva, thank you for being the spark that lit this fire and for inspiring me to continue this journey. I'm grateful every day that I get to be your Papa.

CONTENTS

AUTHOR'S NOTE

In February 2014, my mother was diagnosed with stage 3 lung cancer. For anyone who has had a cancer diagnosis of someone close to them, you are never fully prepared to hear those words from the doctor.

My mother had been a smoker most of her life, and even though a part of me already knew, it still shook me to my core to hear the diagnosis. I carried a lot of guilt that year. My mother lived more than 1,500 miles away, so part of me would feel guilty when I traveled to take care of her, because I wasn't back home. I knew my daughter missed me.

By August of that year, the doctor said the chemo had been doing well, and it looked like we were making some headway against the cancer. In October, it came back even more aggressively and began to spread.

That December, five days before Christmas, she finally lost her fight.

Several months after my mom died, I found myself crying in the bathroom. My daughter must have heard me because she opened the door and looked in.

"What's the matter, Papa?" she asked.

I had grown up believing the message that as a man, I shouldn't ask for help—that I needed to be able to handle it all if I was truly worthy of being called a "man," or else I was weak. In that moment, the old story kicked back in. I unconsciously began wiping my eyes dry as a voice in my head yelled, "Stop crying! Don't let her see you like this. Be strong!"

Then I paused and looked up at her, her eyes filled with concern and love, and something in me shifted. With tears running down my face, I said, "I'm just really sad because I miss grandma."

She walked over to me, put her arms around me, and hugged me, saying, "I miss her too, Papa. I miss her too."

This amazing, beautiful, five-year-old child simply saw who I was at that moment and responded with compassion and empathy. My daughter may not remember this story. I'll never forget it. It was the start of my shift and willingness to stop hiding the grief and hurt that I was feeling and helped me to begin leaning on my world a little more and asking for help.

There is a commonly held belief that men can be providers, protectors, achievers. *Or,* they can be caregivers, nurturing, and in touch with their emotions.

These are <u>not</u> mutually exclusive.

Many men grew up being taught that being vulnerable is a weakness.

They grew up believing that asking for help made them less for some reason; that as a man, you must do it all, you must win and triumph; that only certain emotions are okay for a man to show.

Being happy is okay (though not too happy—don't get full of yourself now). You can be sad (but only for a little while, and then you need to get right back at it!). Anger is okay in limited doses (and, of course, only in certain places and expressed in certain ways). Fear? (Probably best not to let that one show, or others will see you as weak or incapable.) The list goes on.

Those lessons about which emotions are appropriate (or not) are taught and reinforced in movies, television, stories, and often in the examples we see from other men in our lives when we are young boys.

I believe that is a limiting perspective that holds us back—that there is another way forward. Instead of an either/or approach, it must be about both/and. We, as men, can be strong *and* sensitive. We can be independent *and* know there are times in our life when we need to ask for help. We can fiercely protect those we care about *and* nurture and love them with the same measure of ferocity.

My goal is to highlight how this is the way we create greater connection and intimacy with the people in our world.

I spent nine years as an active-duty Infantry Officer in the Marine Corps. Following my time in the Marines, I spent six years in construction. Both careers allowed me to see a lot of how others viewed what masculinity was and what it meant to be a man.

While I was successful, something also didn't feel quite right, and I continually felt like I had to shut parts of myself off in order to show up the way others expected me to be in those roles. In 2015, I began interviewing men around the topic of vulnerability, and in 2020 I launched a podcast called *The Vulnerable Man.*

The podcast was a natural growth and expansion from the conversations I had been having with men. I realized that so many men I was talking to were yearning for more—searching for a way to more openly express and talk about these things and feel safe doing so.

Free from the stigmatism that has them feel like broaching this topic is unmanly.

I believe that we can expand the definition and meaning of masculinity to become more inclusive and allow men to stop having to shut off or hide parts of themselves. This evolution will allow them to embrace more fully who they are naturally, ultimately moving toward a healthier version of what masculinity represents.

While we all can benefit from letting ourselves be a little more vulnerable, regardless of your gender or how you identify, I am focusing this book on men. You will also find value if you have a man in your life that you want to support by better understanding the challenges men face around expressing greater vulnerability.

In the last decade, as I have continued to dive deeper and deeper into this topic of vulnerability, I've been shown increasing instances where men don't feel safe in showing it. I know they are yearning for it, much like I am. They want to be a more authentic and robust version of themselves instead of having to just show certain portions in order to be accepted.

At our core, we are all human, and we can all benefit from creating safety so that others can show up more fully as themselves without fear of judgment, ridicule, or harm.

While my journey is unique to myself, I know that many of the struggles I have faced are similar to the struggles others have gone through. I will be sharing some of my own stories of failure and success throughout this book, along with the stories of other men, as a way to help illustrate the challenges we face around vulnerability.

I am far from perfect and never strive for the ideal of perfection. I'm human. I'm also more committed to bringing this work into the world than I am to my own comfort.

One of my biggest learnings is that when I overcome my fears and share myself by being vulnerable, it creates deeper connections and stronger relationships with the people in my world. It keeps me from being isolated and alone and allows me to show others that doing this is possible.

We must begin focusing on what connects us and what we share in our humanity.

Gentlemen, my hope is that you read this and find something that helps you step a little closer to being vulnerable and letting your world see a little more of who you are. For those reading this who don't identify as male, I hope you can gain some insights into the things that inhibit men from showing greater vulnerability and learn ways to create safe spaces for them to do so in the future.

HOW WE GOT HERE

———

CHAPTER 1

MASCULINITY THROUGH TIME

In Greek mythology, Hercules was famous for his great strength and many adventures. As a young boy fascinated by mythology, I read *The Twelve Labors of Hercules*—these were some of his most well-known feats and helped cement his place in mythological lore. The importance of strength and independence are amplified and especially true in fictitious stories and reflect some of the qualities commonly attributed to "real men."

Whether he was slaying the Nemean lion, getting the girdle of the Queen of the Amazons, or stealing the Mares of Diomedes, he managed to triumph and be victorious. The stories I read created fascinating pictures and imagery in my mind as I pictured him accomplishing these seemingly impossible things.

Throughout recorded history, there has continued to be an aspect of qualifying masculinity by the accomplishments and physical feats of men. It would build a structure that men could be mere mortals, or they could be more—but never at the same time.

Often, specific traits that were praised in men became associated with masculinity, and this is evident as we look at what the twelve main gods from Roman mythology—both male and female—represented.

Male Roman Gods	Female Roman Gods
Jupiter: King of the Gods; God of thunder and lightning.	Juno: Wife of Jupiter; Goddess of women and fertility.
Mars: God of war.	Venus: Goddess of love and beauty.
Mercury: God of travelers and tradesmen.	Diana: Goddess of hunting, archery, and animals.
Neptune: God of the sea.	Minerva: Goddess of wisdom, learning, arts, and industry.
Vulcan: God of blacksmiths and volcanoes.	Ceres: Goddess of agriculture, harvest, and the seasons.
Apollo: God of music, archery, healing, poetry, and truth.	Vesta: Goddess of hearth and home.

I observed that the male gods represented things that have been traditionally associated with masculinity, whereas the female gods represented things that have been traditionally associated with femininity. Both Diana and Apollo represent archery; yet, for the other gods, the division seemed to fall in line with roles traditionally assigned to men and women.

For men, it was war, trade, and blacksmithing; for women, it was love, the arts, and harvest. As a result, it seemed as if when a man wasn't doing things that fell into those traditional norms, they came to be seen as unmanly or more womanlike.

In the narrative, the hero always finds a way to overcome every challenge. Many of these stories had male protagonists.

You'll have a harder time locating well-known ones that have a female main character as this hero archetype. That is shifting more in the last ten to twenty years, though not as commonplace as it needs to become.

The hero's journey always featured some initial setbacks or failures and usually featured doubt about their ability to persevere. Yet, despite any setbacks they encountered, they ultimately triumphed.

This reinforced the idea that heroic men never fail to complete or overcome a challenge. For many young men who struggle and don't succeed, it can build feelings of not being a "real man" by those unrealistic standards.

Many heroes from stories had some kind of mentor or sage who helped them along the way. These were often individuals who held wisdom but didn't possess the strength our hero did. The mentor was a guide along the way yet couldn't accomplish what the hero needed to do. This reinforced the stereotype of the hero needing to go it alone.

Most of the quests the hero undertook were done solo. They may have received help in some places, but the toughest parts of the challenge had to be done themselves. A lot of these mythological stories praised the lone champion who had to struggle before finding a way through.

The hero's journey also implied that if you didn't suffer some hardships and then overcome them, you weren't a man.

Now let me be clear, I believe we learn and grow when we must overcome challenges in our lives; it's a part of growing and developing. That being said, the stories often tied to the hero's journey require almost hypermasculine values or qualities to overcome the challenge, which creates the message that if you can't perform these heroic-level feats, you might not be a true man.

Many such stories imply that you had to "earn" the title of man through some trial, or that the title had to be given to you by another. This concept can be emasculating and put men in a position where they're continually evaluating/comparing themselves to other men or some standard of what a "real man" is.

Inevitably, men were doomed to fall short if they didn't embody the hypermasculine standard that stories like these expected.

Masculinity Heroes in the Media

Much like the characters in mythology, one of the most popular characters I watched on the silver screen while growing up as a kid in the seventies and eighties was James Bond (and before we go any further, let's just get on the same page: Sean Connery is Bond and everyone else is fighting for second place on the podium). I also saw Arnie (*The Terminator, Conan, Commando*). Other actors were also prominent at the time, but these two stood out most for me.

I could talk about others I watched, such as Clint Eastwood (*Dirty Harry*), Chuck Norris, Sylvester Stallone, and Burt Reynolds, but that could fill another entire book. All these fictitious characters possessed a sense of machismo in one way or another, and all of them played off of a very narrow portrayal of masculinity.

These cinema characters reinforced forms of masculinity that were fairly one-dimensional (i.e., get the woman, win, don't show weakness; strength and power are more important than empathy or compassion). Here are some lessons I learned from each:

James Bond

- He was clever and *arrogantly confident* (which often got him into some of the predicaments he would then need to find a way out of). As a result, if I wasn't always completely sure of myself in any situation (and especially when caught in a very elaborate yet easily escapable trap set by a criminal mastermind), then I wasn't a man.
- He always *made women swoon*. As a young boy, I marveled at how women always fell for him, and it wasn't until I was older that I could really see how it sent a very unhealthy message. Even when the women would "resist" him, he would "turn on the Bond charm," and the ladies would end up being seduced by him.

The barely hidden message: even if they say no, keep pursuing. If you're man enough, they'll come around. Having been raised by a single mother, this conflicted with my beliefs and took me time to sort through to fully understand the dangerous message.

Arnold Schwarzenegger (most of his characters)

- Be big and strong. You don't need to use your words when you have more muscles than everyone else.
- Intimidation and brute force will get it done.
- Overcome impossible odds. Real men do, so you better as well.

The message: If you're strong enough, everyone will eventually bend to your will (or be crushed along the way). Real men are physical specimens. Strength trumps intelligence (IQ or EQ).

These characters (and many others) were portrayed to reflect the traits and characteristics that society connected with being a "man," which also emphasized and reinforced many elements of unhealthy masculinity. (More on the idea of healthy and unhealthy masculinity to come in the next chapter... stay tuned!)

Comic Book Superheroes

When I was a kid, I always enjoyed reading comic books. I don't know if it was the element of the character discovering they had some hidden powers, their ability to save the day, or their constant service to others—making their lives a little bit better. It was a way for me to escape from the world for a little while and imagine another reality.

Some of the characters I connected with and enjoyed reading about were Iron Man, Batman, Superman, and Spider-Man. I dug on the X-Men. I also read about the adventures of Conan the Barbarian when they weren't mainstream enough to be labeled as "graphic novels," but that's a story for another book.

While each superhero had their own origin story and motivations for doing what they did, there was usually a theme in how they operated. Each hero would have their own code, and something about that was intriguing to me.

Some of them had powers that had been given to them, while others didn't necessarily possess special skills or abilities. Those without special powers had trained or developed ways to gain capabilities beyond the normal individual.

As that impressionable young boy reading these comics, the unspoken message I learned was that if I wanted to become a superhero, I had to:

- Have a secret identity
  - This taught me there had to be a separation between who heroes were in their hero state and who they were as ordinary people. The two parts could not coexist at the same time. It implied the average guy wasn't capable of being a hero to the outside observer and that only a select few earned that mantle.
- Do it alone
  - The hero doesn't need anyone but himself, so if you can't vanquish your foes, you are inadequate. This reinforced a message that, as men, we must do it alone; we can't reach out and have community.
- Never show weakness or hurt
  - Inevitably, the hero would get hurt in some way, yet he never allowed anyone to see it. Not his enemies lest they use it against him. Certainly not the people you care about because then they'd see you weren't perfect.
- Be physically strong
  - Most heroes used their might to defeat the villain. Look at the way they were drawn—oversized with insanely sculpted muscles. They possessed physiques the average mortal could never achieve, which reinforced the message that strength was a measurement of being a man.

Batman stood out to me as a prime example of how some of these themes hindered who he could fully be as a man. Batman was strong, unbeatable, and relentless—but those exceptional feats were only possible when Bruce Wayne donned the suit. When he wasn't in costume, Bruce suffered as he tried to avoid dealing with the trauma of his past, namely witnessing his parents being murdered in front of him.

Instead of seeking to face that trauma and finding a way to deal with it, he lived the alter ego of Batman as a way of venting the rage and aggression he suppressed in his life as Bruce. He continually kept himself distanced from others, not allowing them to get close or connect with him in a deep way.

Bruce's continued efforts to keep walls around himself played into his belief that he had to do it alone and couldn't rely on others. Before some of you get up in arms—yes, he did have Robin in some adventures. For most of Batman's story, he operated alone, which is where I'm pointing to.

The one person that Bruce did let remain in his life was Alfred, the family's butler. At times, Bruce would push back against Alfred, especially when he would try to appeal to Bruce's humanity and encourage him to connect and trust others more.

One other thing I found interesting was that Alfred was also portrayed in ways that seemed almost opposite to how the masculine narrative typically went. He wasn't physically strong or intimidating. He showed emotions instead of hiding them. He was a caregiver and nurtured Bruce.

It should also be noted that Alfred demonstrated characteristics traditionally associated with the feminine, particularly in the aspect of nurturing and being a caregiver. Alfred was seemingly the antithesis of what a hero should be, yet he was foundational for Bruce's humanity to flourish.

A Hero's Return

As I look at comic book characters now and reflect on how they were when I was a kid, something else that stands out to me is the way they were often drawn and portrayed. Pay close attention, and you will notice they emphasized the obscenely large, defined muscles the heroes possessed. They were almost inhumanly lean and fit.

They were an unrealistic portrayal of what the typical male body looks like.

I don't know if that was by design to help us as mere mortals feel inadequate or separate from the superheroes we idolized. What I do know is that when looking at them, I could never picture myself like that. It seemed unattainable to me.

I would see the image of Superman standing in his classic pose—arms akimbo, chest out, gazing to one side—an image that at once radiated power and confidence. I unconsciously began to think that I could not be like that because I didn't see that same image when I looked in the mirror.

Those individuals represented some form of a man that I could never become. How's that hit you for setting someone up for a lifetime of feelings of inadequacy?

It didn't connect for me then, but as I look back now, I think there may have been an unconscious message playing. You could be a strong and powerful hero, or you could be a mere mortal—a man. But never the two shall coexist.

It carried this idea that you could either present yourself as strong, capable, and able to help others, or you couldn't. It further reinforced this idea surrounding unhealthy masculinity that a man couldn't be strong and still need to ask for help from others.

The superheroes in these comics supposedly represented "the best in us," and if a man couldn't embody the ideals represented by superheroes, he wasn't manly enough.

Masculinity in Western Culture

Toward the end of the nineteenth century, as people began to move west and settle throughout North America, some highly regarded traits of men were the ability to be hardy, to be a pioneer, and to be able to survive hardship in new environments. As the twentieth century rolled around and industrial production began to rise, the emphasis shifted to place importance on a man's ability to be able to work hard and perform in a workplace.

When World War I broke out, the ability to serve his country and defend became a marker for evaluating a man. A similar thing happened again during World War II. Men were expected to provide service to a higher ideal, to the country, and show a willingness to sacrifice for their fellow man and endure the hardships of war and do so without complaining. Men who couldn't serve, or chose not to, were often looked down on.

Don't get me wrong; I am a firm believer in serving. I chose to serve in the Marine Corps and am proud of that service. Where I want to make the distinction is that if we begin to determine a man's value on whether he could serve or does serve, we are missing the mark.

We are holding to a narrow view of what masculinity is about and the ways in which a man might be able to contribute.

As the second half of the twentieth century took place, the civil rights and women's liberation movements began to shift some of the ways that men were viewed, and the ways of what it meant to be a man shifted with it.

The lines between many of the traditional roles or expectations often divided between men and women began to blur. People started questioning the old norms they adhered to. As a result, in the seventies and eighties, an immense movement began where men started shifting and questioning what being a man meant.

In the twenty-first century, men continue to question this idea of what it means to be a man, and now some of the conversation has shifted to look at the ways we view masculinity. A movement has begun which rejects that the only definition is the "type-A alpha male" as the sole measure of a man. This is creating an openness to including other elements that can be part of defining what masculinity means to us today, and it's the first step in how we can begin evolving masculinity.

In the next chapter, we will explore the idea of healthy and unhealthy masculinity—and how we can continue evolving what it means to be a man.

CHAPTER 2

HIDING BEHIND THE MASK

Rites of Passage

Many cultures around the world hold a ceremony or ritual to mark the moment when a boy transitions into manhood. Often, this ritual is symbolic of his individual growth. The ritual often involves some kind of act or challenge that he must accomplish or overcome on his own.

Completion of the ritual represents the transition from boyhood into this new role of manhood. A celebration or ceremonial gathering of the tribe or the family is held to welcome him once his rite of passage is complete.

Following the rite of passage, he is viewed differently and held with new responsibilities in that group. It not only gives the boy new status as a man, but it also reminds him of the responsibilities and expectations that are now placed upon him in his role in his community. It serves as a reminder that he is required to contribute to the group in a greater capacity.

Some include rites of passage that have more than just a physical aspect and include a challenge they must solve with critical thinking. It is meant to help the young man test himself and better understand his limits beyond his physical capabilities.

A tribe in the Amazon requires a boy to place his hand in a woven glove that contains bullet ants (which apparently have the most painful sting of any ant we know of). As a test of his manhood, he must keep his hand in the glove for several minutes without making a sound.

(Oh yeah, and in case you were wondering, he may have to repeat this ritual several more times before he is considered a man. I think I'll take a pass on that one.)

The ancient Spartans trained young boys to become warriors at the age where most of us these days would start sending our kids to elementary school. Upon reaching his eighteenth birthday, the young Spartan would be sent off with a knife to kill the slaves of their enemies. If he could accomplish this while remaining undetected, he would be considered a man and accepted as a member of the Spartan elite.

The Maasai people in Africa would require a young teenage boy to leave the village armed only with a spear as part of his rite of passage. He would have to kill a lion all by himself and bring it back to earn the title of a warrior.

While I don't know that rites of passage such as those listed would serve in our modern times, they held a sense of power and gravity that was an acknowledgment of that young man's transition into manhood. The closest example I can think of is military boot camp. For any who have served, this rite of passage is part of what must be completed to be fully accepted into the larger group.

In 2017, Ron Fritz discussed the idea of coming-of-age rituals and rites of passage in a way that caught my attention. Ron shares how he and his wife created their own version of a rite of passage that was different for their son and their daughter, with each customized to what they wanted to help instill and share with their kids. (Fritz 2017)

One element they created was a challenge to help them lean into resourcefulness. They gave each child a five-dollar bill, and each had five minutes to go into the grocery store to buy items that would protect an egg that was dropped from a second-story window. Where they upped the ante in the challenge? All the things they bought had to be edible. (You'll have to watch Ron's talk to find out how it went.)

I loved the concept of creating this rite of passage, and I'm contemplating what I'd like to do for my own daughter as she approaches her teenage years.

In many of the rites of passage, the boys were encouraged to demonstrate their ability to endure touch challenges. Not just endure, but also do so without letting others see how hard it may have been. Not showing emotion or limiting the ones they let others see was a common thread, and I believe this reinforced a framework of masculinity that no longer serves.

What keeps us as men from stepping away from this outdated model of masculinity? What are the factors that have us continue to hide parts of ourselves and avoid embracing a fuller expression of being a man? That's where we are going next as we explore some of the primary things that keep men hiding behind a mask.

Emotions are Emotions

In an article from the early 1970s entitled "Universal Facial Expressions of Emotion," an American psychologist by the name of Paul Ekman—who studied nonverbal communication—identified six basic emotions people in all human cultures experienced, shown through facial expressions. These were:

- Joy (happiness)
- Loneliness (sadness)
- Grossness (disgust)
- Fear
- Shock (surprise)
- Wrath (anger)

He went on years later to add more to the list, though we'll focus on the core six he started with.

At their core, emotions are neither good nor bad. They are simply emotions.

How we choose to respond and behave because of the emotions we experience is where we begin to assign positive and negative labels. We have assigned the positive and negative attributes to them as a way of categorizing, which is part of what our brains love to do.

The danger is that this is a fallacy. If I experience anger yet do nothing as a result, how is it something negative? That anger can be an indicator to me that some boundary of mine is being pushed up against, or that a value of mine may be getting ignored or stepped on.

An article published by the Canadian Mental Health Association (https://cmha.ca/what-if-negative-emotions-arent-so-bad/) talks about some of the myths and facts surrounding anger and sadness.

Anger

Myth: Anger serves no constructive purpose.

Fact: Anger can actually be our friend when we're not acting it out.

When it is justified and appropriate, anger can be constructive. It can help clarify and solve problems and correct misunderstandings in relationships. When people can express their anger calmly, they are more able to resolve conflict. Some researchers suggest that constructive anger can even promote heart health.

When we are threatened or attacked, anger can provide the strength we need to protect ourselves or stand our ground. Social movements fueled by anger can also be effective in overcoming injustice in society.

Sadness

Myth: Sadness serves no purpose.

Fact: In many cultures, sadness is considered an "undesirable" or "problem" emotion that serves no purpose. In fact, sadness serves important functions. Sadness can trigger thinking and behavior strategies that help us deal with demanding social situations. It is also a healthy way to process an experience of loss.

Trying to suppress or ignore them only makes them take up more space. Suppressing certain emotions (e.g., sadness or anger) also serves to numb us and reduce our emotional range. What we don't realize is that trying to minimize our "lows" also has the effect of limiting how high our "highs" can be.

Think of a beach ball. If you hold it underwater, it will want to pop back up to the surface. If you hold it just a few inches below the water's surface, it will only rise a small distance above when you let it go. As you try to hold the beach ball deeper, it becomes harder to keep it under. When you finally release it, it pops much higher—usually with much greater force.

When we limit how "low" we allow ourselves to go, it also limits how high we can go when we feel what we deem the "good" or "positive" emotions. We fool ourselves into believing that suppressing those lows serves us, yet it stops us from more deeply riding those highs.

All our emotions start to become muted and numbed, and we slowly creep toward flatlining.

The way to prevent this is to learn how to be with our emotions and process them in a healthy way. When we can experience our emotions, they tend to move through us more readily, and we do not become run by them or held hostage by them.

An article by Tori Rodriguez, published in *Scientific American*, states:

> "anger and sadness are an important part of life, and new research shows that experiencing and accepting such emotions are vital to our mental health." (Rodriguez)

We also need to learn how to have emotions and not let them control us. There is a distinct difference between being angry and then having all our actions result from it. When we can recognize when we are angry, it gives us the ability to be with it and not be in it and overrun by it.

We need to teach children some skills at an early age so they are better prepared as young adults and teenagers. Many adults never learned how to do this properly and could benefit from these skills as well (though I don't know how much they'd be willing to learn at this point).

In North American culture, we have done a poor job of teaching young boys the skills needed to experience and process their emotions. As a result, we continue to create generations of men who don't have the ability to be with their emotions.

This causes them to suppress emotions and put a lid on them—like they are being put in a pressure cooker. Eventually, the pressure grows beyond the capacity to hold them, and those suppressed emotions come exploding out in ways that aren't healthy for the man or those around him.

Limiting Our Emotional Bandwidth

A lot of men I have talked to or interacted with have shared that they feel as if they have to limit the depth of some emotions they show or completely suppress them in order for them to be seen and accepted as men. They struggle with continually gauging how much or how little they should show based on the situation and the people involved.

The unfortunate truth about this is that **these behaviors are ingrained in them at an early age.**

Boys and girls as young children are often quite comfortable expressing many, if not all, of their emotions. Anyone who has spent time around a toddler can attest to this. In the span of a few minutes, a little kid can go from joy to anger, to frustration, to sadness, and back to joy faster than the speed of light. This can be frustrating for the kids themselves just as much as for the adults around them.

For these young children, learning to recognize and process the flood of emotions that go through them can be disruptive, but it is also an important step. At our core, humans are emotional creatures. We all experience emotions; it is part of our human existence.

We start seeing subtle changes happen around the age of four or five. Those same children who are learning how to process and be with their emotions begin to receive different messages on how they should handle their emotions. Either explicitly or subtly, boys frequently begin hearing the message that some emotions are "okay" and others aren't.

If you see a six-year-old boy and a six-year-old girl crying, what message do they each get?

The girl is likely told it is okay for her to cry, and the behavior and processing of her emotions are normalized.

For the little boy, the message is often very different: he hears things like, "toughen up," "don't be a girl," or "shake it off." These messages tend to come from well-intended men (who likely heard the same messages when they were children experiencing these emotions, and as a result, they continue with what they know or were taught).

The unintended impact of these types of messages is that, for boys, certain emotions aren't okay to show, and if you have them, you'd better get over them quickly. And above all else, don't let yourself feel the emotions and experience them; you need to control and minimize them instead.

The most common emotions that young boys hear these lessons around are sadness, anger, and frustration. The boys begin telling themselves they must suppress or hide them in order to be seen as "manly." They avoid the emotions that aren't considered good ones. As a result, they begin to minimize when those feelings do show up.

The minimizing or avoidance is then rewarded by the male role models in their life, which reinforces the suppressive behavior around emotions. They become conditioned to avoid what are labeled the "bad" emotions, and they can't learn how to process them. Continual suppression or avoidance leads to problems down the road when these bottled-up emotions burst out in unhealthy ways.

One other place where boys get messaging that encourages them to hide or suppress emotions is in video games. Ashly Burch said: [https://youtu.be/6fh_ZPc29ks]

> "Violent videogames reinforce the stereotypical structures of what a man should be. The typical game characters tend to be white males with, it gets this specific, brunette hair, five o'clock shadow. When an emotion sneaks in for a male character, by and large it is anger, and any sort of grief is underplayed and never actually discussed or processed. Kids end up really looking up to this character and what they end up idolizing is someone who cannot express themselves emotionally, cannot be honest or open with anyone around them."

Considering how prevalent video games are in our current culture, there is a high volume of this message for boys that the real heroes and manly men who win are the ones who are closed off and dominate through force. This can also create elements of shame for boys who might not see themselves as those video game characters.

Shaming

In 2016, I began interviewing men around this subject of vulnerability to better understand how others viewed the word. In the casual conversations I had been having with men up to that point, I noticed some similarities regarding how they responded to the idea of being vulnerable, regardless of how we got onto the subject.

The interviews consisted of five questions centered around better understanding what got in the way of men feeling safe in being more vulnerable. While doing these interviews, I discovered how men viewed themselves and how they measured themselves as to whether they met the standard of what it meant to "be a man."

One question, in particular, focused on what got in the way of them being vulnerable around or with other men. In some of the conversations, I found that many of them said they were able to show some level of openness with their female partners / significant others, yet when it came to talking about deeper conversations with other men, the topics tended to be shallower or not as open.

As I spoke with more and more men, I noticed their answers fell into one of three categories, all of which shared a direct link with the idea of shame.

- Judgment and External Expectations
- Past Experiences
- Self-Acceptance and Self-Esteem

The judgment and external expectations centered around concerns about being perceived as weak or "less than." The men would say things like they hesitated in showing greater vulnerability because of unspoken expectations around how a man was supposed to show up and act. Several of them made comments like, "men shouldn't have to ask for help," or, "I can't cry as a man; it's not manly."

The judgment became even stronger when they spoke about a working or professional setting. Where some men expressed willingness to be more open at home, very few felt comfortable doing so in a work setting. They felt the expectations were even more strict in those professional settings and felt there was no room for them to show emotions. If they did show emotions, they were limited to a few, such as frustration, anger, or joy.

One observation that I had never considered before came from a man who identifies as gay. He said that one reason he felt hesitant to be more open with men was because of a concern that it would be received as some sort of come-on by another man who identified as straight. He admitted it was what he called his "own internalized homophobia" and that because of it, he held back so he wouldn't risk making other men feel uncomfortable.

Past experiences played a big part in whether these men carried shame. The men whose past vulnerability was not well received—met with ridicule or ostracization—became wary of opening up around other men in the future. Some of the men shared that when they saw examples of other men demonstrating vulnerability, it made them personally uncomfortable.

For the men who had more accepting responses when they opened up, it tended to reduce the feeling of shame and then emboldened them to be more open, particularly in their interactions with other men.

A smaller group of men had mixed responses when they let their guards down and opened up, and they remained willing to their commitment to being open more in the future. They did not allow those negative experiences to dissuade them from continuing their own path.

Self-acceptance and self-esteem were the bridge between external expectations and past experiences. The men who had higher levels of each had greater resilience to bad experiences, and they tended to be more forgiving of themselves. They held self-compassion when men reacted negatively to their vulnerability.

The role models these men had while growing up also played heavily into how the men did or didn't continue to hide behind masks. Unsurprisingly, many men shared with me that they rarely (if ever) saw their own fathers cry or show a lot of emotion. And through that, they began to develop the unspoken belief that men are not emotional creatures.

For the men who had examples of men who were able to be more open and vulnerable, they developed a greater sense of willingness to do so themselves. They also didn't withdraw as much if that openness was poorly received or even rejected by other men.

An incredible documentary created by The Representation Project called *The Mask You Live In* was released in 2015. When I first watched it, it was like everything fell into place for me. I had been struggling to understand why I was feeling challenged with some of the messaging I had been hearing as a man (along with the messaging that carried over from my childhood) about being a man—and this clarified where the disconnect was for me.

I began seeing through some of the stereotypes of masculinity that were built up for me playing football and basketball as a young boy—how the sense of competition was glorified, and domination and winning were made the focus. The young boys that were praised were the ones who didn't cry or those who brushed off pain and hurt. The coaches who would make comments like "don't be a girl" or "suck it up" would unconsciously (and I hope unintentionally) encourage us to shy away from those qualities that were seen as effeminate.

We are starting to see a shift in men; they are fed up with this old approach of having to limit themselves and their ability to show emotion. The fact that you are reading this book gives me hope that we can continue to normalize men connecting with and expressing emotion without fear of judgment.

In the next chapter, we are going to look at how everything we've discussed to this point can be used to better define healthy and unhealthy masculinity and how we can create space for more healthy masculinity to emerge.

CHAPTER 3

HEALTHY AND UNHEALTHY MASCULINITY

———

A few months before my daughter was born, I took a course called Boot Camp for New Dads (BCND). Greg and Alison Bishop created it, and they designed it for men who were about to become fathers for the first time. That three-hour workshop was a catalyst for change regarding my definition of what it meant to be a man and was the most powerful three hours I spent in my preparation for becoming a dad.

I witnessed Veteran Dads (the ones in the room with their own babies) talking to the Rookie Dads (the expectant fathers) about the challenges and lessons they had learned. Most importantly, I saw those Vet Dads being fathers. They changed diapers, dealt with crying babies, and emanated confidence in their roles, which inspired me.

Until that point, most of the examples I had seen of fatherhood were on TV or in the movies, and I certainly hadn't seen men actively engaged in these types of activities with the dedication and love that the Vet Dads showed.

When I thought back to many of the dads I had seen on TV as a young boy or teenager, many were portrayed as goofy, aloof, and awkward when it came to caretaking. You often knew they cared about their children, and rarely did the storylines show dads being fathers like I saw at BCND.

Seeing those Veteran Dads in action confirmed to me my desire to be active and involved in all aspects of fatherhood, not just the traditionally viewed ones. Yes, I wanted to be a provider and protector, and I also wanted to be a nurturer and caregiver.

When I began evolving and growing my perspective of masculinity, it gave rise to a powerful moment.

Evolution

Evolving masculinity is about looking at the parts that have worked and are still needed as we go forward.

It includes being willing to let go of what isn't needed, and it is about evolving and adding to how we hold it / see it. It is not simply erasing what has been created around the idea of masculinity.

One of the definitions of evolution is: "A process of change in a certain direction." This fits best with the vision I hold.

When I think of evolution, it includes the idea of an organism or entity adapting to its environment in a way that will help it better survive and thrive going forward. It does not automatically mean that everything that it was before is removed. Instead, it keeps the aspects that are needed and begins to develop new elements to enable growth in the current or future environment.

The human race evolved into our current form based upon the needs of the environment, and it is time for the same kind of evolution to take place around masculinity.

Themaneffect.com defines masculinity as:

> Standards of manliness or masculinity vary across different cultures and historical periods. Traits traditionally viewed as masculine in Western society include strength, courage, independence, leadership, and assertiveness.

I want to focus on the last part of this one. The traits of "strength, courage, independence, leadership, and assertiveness." I am not going to dissect each of these, though I do want to take a moment to look at three that I think have become overblown and are continuing to uphold this idea of unhealthy masculinity in our time.

Moving from "Either/Or" to "Both/And"

Many elements of strength, independence, and assertiveness have helped the idea of masculinity in healthy and positive ways. Just like any trait, there can be shadow and light sides to it. And any trait, when overdone, can lead to negative impacts and results.

For example, if I display confidence, it can come across in a positive way. If I overdo it, it might be received as arrogance or conceit.

Therefore, I hold on to the idea of *evolving* masculinity. I believe looking at which parts, when they're used proportionately, can benefit and serve humanity is essential.

Equally, we need to look at where some of these traits leave room to expand or change.

For example, we must begin to grow the narrative around strength to include the aspect of emotional strength—of giving men the permission to be able to display their emotions more freely and without fear of their psychological safety in doing so.

Making it safe for them to show this different type of strength and allowing them to say they are struggling without it creating a stigma is imperative. We can reinforce this by acknowledging how they are demonstrating courage when they own that they can't do something alone and by teaching them that asking for help isn't a sign of weakness. It will normalize the behavior and invite more of it in the future.

In one of the coach training courses I was leading recently, I performed a coaching demonstration with one of the participants. As we worked together, he opened up, found his way to a very vulnerable place, and got emotional. When the coaching was complete, several participants acknowledged how powerful it was to see him be open like that and how it had inspired them. He shared with me later in the day that hearing that from his peers gave him more confidence to be more vulnerable in other areas of his life.

We must start looking at masculinity through the lens of what is needed both today and in the future to better serve humanity. The simple truth is that there is no longer one perfect way to define masculinity. Our world is changing and continues to change. How we hold masculinity needs to change and evolve as well to meet those needs.

It is not an "either/or" approach to masculinity. It is "both/and."

Not either I'm strong and independent, *or* I'm caring and compassionate.

I'm confident, *or* I'm afraid something won't work out.

I work hard, *or* I'm a good husband/father/partner.

Find a middle ground between these extremes and know there are many gradations in between where masculinity can exist and thrive.

We often get trapped in this extreme view of it having to be one or the other. When we look at many examples of masculinity, it highlights one or the other and doesn't show the grey space in between.

As men, we get tricked into believing that we must pick one of these two options—that they are the only choices we have. It's a fool's choice that we continue to reinforce. Whether this is a trap we have created ourselves or one we have allowed to be created does not matter anymore.

When we think there are only two options, we feel limited, and we can only see those options as ways out. The reality is that neither of those two holds the answer to getting us to where we need to go.

Stopping for a moment and recognizing that there are more than just these extremes available to us is what will help us get to the next level and begin to evolve masculinity.

We need to look for and showcase examples of men that hold both as possible in the same space and at the same time. Show the examples in TV, movies, magazines, and newspapers where a man can be confident and still have some fear, where he can work hard and be a good husband or father or partner—where he can be successful and still fail sometimes.

When men and young boys start seeing these examples, we will start shifting the narrative and allowing others to begin seeing possibility as well beyond just the fool's choice we feel trapped in.

I began this chapter by talking about some of the dads I saw on TV while I was growing up. More recently, some characters who model this new narrative are Randall Pearson from *This Is Us* and Phil Dunphy from *Modern Family*. Their love for their children is ever apparent, and we also see them walking the middle ground and being in that "both/and" space.

Strength.

If we look at stereotypical portrayals of strength from this masculine viewpoint, it brings the idea of not just physical strength but also psychological strength. "Real men" can overpower. They can push through. They can bear any burden placed upon them.

I entered "strength+men" into the Google search bar, and the *first three pages* of what it found all related to *physical* strength.

From questions about how much to bench press, to offering workout routines, to plenty of ads for a bunch of supplements that will help me "get ripped fast!" (And, of course, now I have a bunch of pop-up nutrition ads appearing on my web browser page, even though I never clicked on any of them.)

If you look at images associated with that search, you get a picture of a bunch of shirtless guys in various poses showing off all their bulging muscles. This continues to expand this image for boys that to be a man, they need to have these overdone physiques in order to measure up.

In my conversation with Josh Levs on *The Vulnerable Man* podcast, we talk about how this impacts young men, and he mentions the idea of "bigorexia" that some men fall victim to. Josh shared,

> That story came from me learning about how even little boys were having body image crises, even at age five and six, feeling that they're too thin and not muscular enough. And I started talking with all these doctors and looking at the research and found that boys are messing with their bodies in very dangerous ways and taking all kinds of chemicals to try to get these impossibly shaped bodies from what they see in cartoons and certain famous people, you know, like the Rock or whatever. And human beings do not take on those forms in nature.

So this is an entire phenomenon that's getting almost no attention because people hear "body image" and they just think of girls, and girls in the body image process. That is very important and must be addressed, but that never means ignoring the fact that boys and men are experiencing it too. (Veal 2022)

For the heck of it, I also looked up "strong man" (consciously aware of putting the space in between the two words). Google was having none of that and, of course, brought up images of Strongmen competitors over the years.

Awesome. As if I wasn't already aware that it's been longer than I care to admit since I've been to the gym, I have all these other men named Chris (Chris Evans, Chris Hemsworth, and Chris Pratt, for example) staring back at me from my computer display with a look that seems to ask, "Why aren't you buff like us, Christopher?"

It was at least four pages into that last search before I found a single link that didn't refer to physical strength.

My point in this is that we have created and perpetuated a belief that strength for men is solely focused on the physical aspect, and it ignores or doesn't allow space for strength to include more.

Independence.

"Real men" don't need help; they do it alone.

Think of your favorite action hero movie scene. The lone hero battles countless, heavily armed bad guys and somehow beats them all, single-handedly. (Not only does our hero have the Hollywood ammo that never runs out, but they also never seem to miss their target!) He never needs anyone to help him.

How about superhero movies? Similar examples. While some of the recent ensemble movies have them teaming up, they still include elements where one or more of the characters goes off on their own to battle their inner demons/ghosts before rejoining the team.

This message of having to do it solo continues to reinforce the narrative that independence is a key measure of being a man.

We hear things growing up as boys and young men that say we shouldn't need to ask for help; we should figure it out on our own.

We hear that asking for help is a sign of weakness.

We live in a society that largely rewards us for individualism. Our education systems are structured around competition. The goal is to get the top grades so you can get into the right school and then follow the right career path and buy the right house/car/etc. You can see where I'm going.

We hear stories about "rags to riches" entrepreneurs who became successful all on their own when the world was against them. We highlight the stories of people braving all odds on their own and coming out victorious on the other end. The message is that as men, we need to be able to do it ourselves, or else we've failed to live up to some unspoken yet agreed-upon standard of masculinity.

It keeps us *isolated* and *alone*.

Assertiveness.

Assertiveness is about not taking no for an answer. "Bold" and "confidence" are some of the first words in its definition. It implies that you must take charge, know where you're going, and not let anything stop you on the way (which also pulls in some of the strength and independence previously discussed). There is very forward-focused energy to it, alongside a sense of powering through or overpowering as well.

Some synonyms of assertive are aggressive, fierce, and in-your-face. They carry the idea of an almost overbearing approach and seem domineering.

Antonyms include low-pressure, unambitious, and unenterprising. When I see these words, it conveys that if you aren't aggressive, you don't want to achieve anything. You can't overcome or be victorious; you're inferior.

In order to be able to move toward a healthier definition of masculinity, we also need to be able to let go of the parts that aren't working.

Tying It All Together

The old paradigm of masculinity tied to strength, independence, and assertiveness as the true measure of manhood ties us to what I consider unhealthy masculinity.

Unhealthy masculinity holds men back. It has us assessing our value as men in terms of how well we perform in sports, how successful we are at work, how many sexual conquests we have, how much we can bench at the gym. It has us look at a very narrow set of criteria and traps us in the outdated either/or thinking of the past.

It also holds us in continual evaluation against other men —continually comparing how we measure up to external factors. It is an unspoken, ever-present dick-measuring contest we are perpetually caught in that nobody can ever win.

Healthy Masculinity embraces that the way we define masculinity is *expansive* and *inclusive*.

It takes elements from how we currently hold it and is open to bringing more into that definition, coming from that "both/and" approach. It values strength and knows it is measured in more than our muscles or how much you can endure. Strength is also about showing compassion and vulnerability—for ourselves as well as others.

It knows that a man can be independent and still be able to say he can't do something, that he needs help sometimes. Healthy masculinity recognizes that asking for help does not equate to weakness or inability to do something.

On any given day, our "best" will vary. What it looks like today or a week or a month or a year from now can change. And that's okay.

Healthy masculinity knows there is a time and place for a man to assert himself. It knows assertiveness for the sake of itself doesn't serve either. Sometimes a man must assert for what he needs yet is afraid to ask for it because of a societal perception that men shouldn't need help or ask for those things. This is especially true in asking for help when he is struggling.

It must show up as asserting and speaking up when other men act in ways that reinforce unhealthy masculinity, even at the risk of losing favor and not "being one of the guys." When we don't speak up, our silence is an unspoken affirmation of that toxic behavior and keeps us from evolving.

We have begun seeing more and more examples of healthy masculinity showing up. Podcasts and books are being created around this topic with a frequency that hasn't happened before.

More men are open to discussing the topic and are sharing that they are hungry for this evolution of masculinity to take place. Men are collectively yearning to be able to step into more of who they are, and we are on the brink of creating a new way to expand what it means to be a man. It's an exciting opportunity unfolding.

In the next chapter, we are going to explore the concept of the Whole Man, and how it can be a way to bring forth more healthy masculinity and vulnerability.

CHAPTER 4

THE WHOLE MAN

A couple of years ago, I started introducing my daughter to the Marvel movies and the comic book characters I grew up reading about as a kid. She took to them like I suspected she would (insert proud Papa smile here). One morning when I was driving her to school, she asked me which superpower I would pick if I could have one.

To me, that was a no-brainer: flight—every day of the week and twice on Sunday. The idea of soaring through the heavens always creates wonder and amazement in me. She chose to have the powers of Dr. Strange (essentially really cool magic abilities) or Captain Marvel (who is a badass woman with enhanced strength, the ability to fly, and can travel throughout the universe at will). I gotta give her credit; those were some good picks that had me rethinking my initial response.

When I was a little boy, I remember taking a towel or a sheet and tying it around my neck. Then I would run around in the yard or the house pretending I was soaring through the sky. My imagination took me to different places as I floated high above the ground in my mind's eye. That cape enabled me to become my own superhero and transform. It allowed me to be free.

Vulnerability

The one true superpower of the Whole Man is *vulnerability*.

Vulnerability allows us to connect and see the humanity in others. It helps us to show who we are and accept who we are in the face of our world and our lives. It is one of the universal things that we as humans know and can experience. And when we allow ourselves to show more of it, we invite people closer.

My own journey toward it has not been an easy path. I traveled it kicking and screaming, dragged along the way many times. Those times when I did fight were only hard because I made it hard.

As I learned to surrender more and let it come forth from me, it became easier and easier.

One of the other things that it can bring is greater intimacy. I don't mean intimacy in the commercialized sense that we often get sold. This definition from the book *Counseling Individuals Through the Lifespan* does a solid job of capturing how I view it:

Intimacy involves the feeling of being in a close, personal association and belonging together. It is a familiar and very close affective connection with another as a result of a bond that is formed through knowledge and experience of the other." (Wong 2014)

I remember subscribing to a different version of intimacy before I started on my journey of exploring my relationship with vulnerability. I had linked it with the idea of a romantic or physical relationship and, like many others, often associated it with sex. A shift around this happened for me when I was in a training course, and a colleague I greatly respected reframed the word intimacy into:

"Into-me-see"

It changed it into an invitation to allow someone to see into you and who you truly were—beyond the external façade we put on, seeing beyond the armor we wear—inviting them in to connect with your humanity.

Letting someone see into you in that way is one of the most vulnerable acts I have experienced. When I have been on the other side, and someone has invited me in to see them in that way, it has been one of the most beautiful gifts I have ever received.

Intimacy is actively cocreated between two or more people. It is not given or received. It takes a conscious decision and desire to create true intimacy.

For men, linking these two is particularly challenging because it generates a fear that if we open up and express a desire for deeper intimacy, it can be equated with a sexual desire. Interacting with other men can trigger responses like homophobia, which ultimately causes men to remain closed and separated from the greater connection they crave.

I know for myself that I tended to shy away from talking about intimacy with others, especially with men, for fear that it would be interpreted in a different way.

The Perception Conundrum

The cape I put on as a kid made me feel invulnerable—like nothing could hurt me. It helped me feel powerful. The funny thing is that as I got older, I began to understand that true power came from the opposite of what I thought as a kid.

Things in life would hurt me… that can't be avoided. I began to derive my power in the moments where I was strong enough to share that I was hurt, that I wasn't invulnerable, that I didn't need to be invulnerable to be whole.

That imagined invulnerability just created a scared little boy on the inside.

In reality, my vulnerability and my openness to being hurt was the real power I had, and it didn't just exist in my mind. As I began to be more open and vulnerable with other men, their show of support encouraged me. Where that scared little boy inside tried to convince me that sharing my hurt would only allow others to hurt me more, the men I spoke with proved that voice wrong.

Shortly after I started going to therapy for the first time, an old college buddy of mine had reached out to connect because he was going to be in town. We met up to grab some food. As we chatted about where life had taken us since our time together at school, I mentioned that while things had been going well overall, I felt overwhelmed and was seeing a therapist.

He said, "I don't know exactly what you're going through, and I'm grateful that I found an amazing therapist for myself three years ago. It was a lifesaver being able to talk about things in that setting." His normalizing of something I believed was scary helped me recognize that sharing my struggle brought us closer together in that moment.

It helped me find more courage to continue sharing and being more open with other men as well.

I have been interviewing men since 2016 around the subject of vulnerability. One of the questions I ask is: "What gets in the way of you being more vulnerable and, in particular, being more vulnerable with other men?" The particulars of their responses vary, but all of them fall under one of these four common themes:

- Judgment
- Fear
- Shame
- Ignorance

Judgment—being seen as "less than" or perceived as weak by society and other men specifically

What I find ironic when it comes to judgment is how these men hold different views depending on how we're talking about it. They often expressed concern that other men might think of them weak, not a man, or not tough enough to handle problems themselves. Then I asked how they would view another friend of theirs who came up and shared something he was struggling with.

Every one of them shared some variation of the fact that they would have respect or appreciation for that man for being open. Not even one mentioned that they would think that man was "less than" or weak for showing vulnerability.

Then I would just sit back and wait. I could see the wheels turning for them and hear the moment when the realization hit them. They recognize they have held vulnerability as something of a liability when they view it in themselves, yet they see it as an asset in others.

Fear—worrying that others will take advantage of or use what they've said against them if they open themselves up

We all are afraid at some point in our lives. It is a part of being human and living. I am not going to propose I have some magic elixir that will make fear disappear forever. From the men that I have interviewed and spoken with over the years, one common thing they share that has helped them be more open is courage.

Courage is not an absence of fear; it is a willingness to move forward in the face of fear.

Having courage means having the insight that the thing you are striving for is more important than letting yourself be held in place by the concern that you might fail.

The possibility is very real that when we allow ourselves to be open and allow people to see into us, they may use that information to hurt us—that they take our words and actions and use them as a weapon. I wish it were otherwise, but it's not. I have come to learn that if I continue living in fear of that happening, I will never truly be myself and be open.

Knowing that the possibility of deeper connection and greater intimacy can be achieved when I let myself be more vulnerable is what helps me find the courage to keep going.

Shame—they have opened up and been rejected or "made wrong" for doing so

Shame is a powerful force that keeps us from being open and whole. It causes us to withdraw and isolate, to keep ourselves separate from others. Shame is an internally driven dialogue that we often play over and over without being aware of it. We have all experienced it in some shape or form in our lives.

A 2016 article from The Good Men Project entitled "The Subtle Shaming of Men and Vulnerability" sums up the struggle a lot of men feel:

The message many men receive is, "Please share yourself with me, but don't share too much or in a way that makes me feel like you're not a strong, confident man." (The Good Men Project 2016)

When it comes to shame, the message men often tell themselves that prevents them from being more open is: if they act vulnerably, they are not strong or confident.

Ignorance—they don't know how to be more vulnerable, or they haven't been shown ways to do so

The last of the common themes is ignorance. I have spoken to many men who talk about the absence of a male role model who expressed elements of vulnerability. Many spoke of examples of fathers, uncles, or grandfathers who were good men and doing the best they could, based on what they knew. Yet, they often (and unconsciously) operated from places of unhealthy masculinity.

The number of men who have mentioned seeing their fathers cry or show deep emotion on a regular basis is far smaller than those who didn't. The examples they were shown had a great influence, positively or negatively, on how that next generation of men viewed being open and in touch with their emotions.

My hope is that this book will help address the last area. By sharing my story and the stories of men that I have encountered, I want to help men be able to find their way to being more vulnerable—to embrace healthy masculinity.

To become a Whole Man.

Expanding the Conversation

In May 2020, while the world was still settling into the growing uncertainty of the pandemic, I recognized I loved the opportunity to talk with men individually about vulnerability through my one-on-one interviews.

One Monday morning, I was interviewing someone, and halfway through the interview, a voice inside me spoke up and said these one-on-one conversations weren't enough.

I was having deep and powerful conversations with these men, yet I was the only one hearing their stories. I knew that if I really wanted to expand the impact and reach of these conversations and help men hear more examples of men being vulnerable, I needed to expand the conversation.

I decided I would start a podcast to help highlight the struggles and triumphs of men finding their way along this journey of vulnerability.

I had no idea where to begin or how to create a podcast. So, I did the vulnerable thing and reached out to my network, asking for assistance. My podcasting guardian angel, Dan Klass, stepped up and generously shared his knowledge, and in July that year, *The Vulnerable Man* podcast was born.

The podcast is part of my work to destigmatize the word vulnerability for men, so they can better connect with themselves and their world. It highlights their journeys and experiences, their successes and failures, and deepens the question of how we view masculinity in our current world.

One of the unexpected gifts and surprises from the podcast is that I have a number of women reaching out to me telling me they want to share my podcast with a man in their life—a husband or boyfriend, even a father or brother. One woman, a single mother, told me that listening to my podcast is shifting the way she is thinking about the intersection of vulnerability and masculinity as she is raising her son. That acknowledgment hit me in the feels.

While I started the podcast knowing that I wanted to talk to men about this subject and expand the way we talk about it, I began to realize that women want to be part of the conversation too. For us to bring about great and meaningful change, we will need to bring men and women together to be in dialogue about how we collectively evolve masculinity.

One final thing that has been a blessing in this journey is that by talking to more men, I subsequently found even more out there to have conversations with. I've been able to connect with men doing similar work to advance the narrative of masculinity, and that has grown my community.

That is a continual reminder for me that the fear I felt before—that had me wanting to isolate and keep small, not playing bigger and expanding—would have kept me from this important work.

Donning our CAPES

In our careers, we wear uniforms as we step up to perform. I wore a very specific one during my nine years on active duty in the Marine Corps. My uniform changed when I transitioned into the corporate world. You wear some form of a uniform in your job even if it is not issued to you. You dress in a certain way to help prepare you for what you need to do.

The Whole Man is no different. With vulnerability as his superpower, he must don his superhero suit to fully embrace it. That means putting on our CAPES, which are the tenets that the Whole Man lives and operates by in all aspects of his life:

Curiosity—a question or wondering and an openness to explore.

Awareness—recognizing where you are and where you need to go.

Presence—slowing down and connecting, filtering out distractions.

Emotional Health—building and sustaining emotional well-being.

Stay—remaining, doing the work, and not running when it gets hard.

I call them the Habits of the Whole Man. The next several chapters will walk through what each of these entails and how you can access them and bring them more fully into your life. The result will allow you to step into a healthier perspective on masculinity and have richer and more rewarding relationships.

And if you want to take that towel or sheet and run around the house while you're reading the book, go for it. I'm not going to judge you.

I know the little boy in me is still wearing his cape.

HABITS OF THE WHOLE MAN (CAPES)

CHAPTER 5

CURIOSITY

One of the basic skills I learned during my time in the Marines is how to navigate using a map and compass. Yes, we have high-tech GPS equipment, but because technology can be fallible, you must know how to get from here to there with nothing more than a map and compass.

Part of navigating includes knowing where you are and where you want to go. You take a heading and set off. Things will cause you to veer off that course: terrain (as much as I'd like to walk straight through that mountain, I will have to go around), natural and man-made obstacles. The list goes on.

When you encounter those things that take you off course, you check in again. "Where am I now? Where is that in relation to where I want to go?" Then you set a new heading and continue. Eventually, with each shift, you find yourself at your destination, or not (more to come on this).

Curiosity operates in much the same way.

My curiosity piqued around the subject of masculinity—and particularly how vulnerability played into it—when I happened across Brené Brown's "The Power of Vulnerability" talk from 2012.

I still remember the first time I watched it. I felt confused and disoriented. Particularly when she spoke about how we numb ourselves and how we cannot selectively numb emotions. On some deep yet seemingly unconscious level, I knew that there was an important message for me to explore here. My head kept trying to wrap itself around her words with minor success, yet instinctually my body knew the message that had to be heard.

This was the first time I had heard someone talk in such a public way about the topic of vulnerability, and I realized that I was curious to know more—especially about where I was resisting my own vulnerability.

That led me to her second talk, "Listening to Shame," which really opened me up. This was one of the first times I looked deeply at some of the differences in the way men were expected to behave and carry themselves. In a particular section near the end of the talk, she shares an exchange she had at one of her book signings:

> For men, shame is not a bunch of competing, conflicting expectations. Shame is one: do not be perceived as what? Weak. I did not interview men for the first four years of my study. It wasn't until a man looked at me after a book signing and said, "I love what you say about shame, I'm curious why you didn't mention men." And I said, "I don't study men." And he said, "That's convenient."
>
> And I said, "Why?" And he said, "Because you say to reach out, tell our story, be vulnerable. But you see those books you just signed for my wife and my three daughters?" I said, "Yeah." "They'd rather me die on top of my white horse than watch me fall down. When

we reach out and be vulnerable, we get the shit beat out of us. And don't tell me it's from the guys and the coaches and the dads, because the women in my life are harder on me than anyone else." (Brown 2012)

Mic drop right there. That short exchange summed up many of the feelings I had experienced in previous relationships. Whether spoken or unspoken, messaging throughout my life told me I couldn't be vulnerable—especially in relationships. I had to be that knight up on that horse who doesn't falter.

Now I began understanding that messaging was a false narrative, and I could start exploring a new story.

For the Whole Man, it all starts with *curiosity*.

Curiosity begins with a question. It is a wondering—an unknowing that sparks the desire to discover or learn. It can show up in many different ways and will usually keep coming up for you until you start to pay attention to it. It may be around a certain topic or word, and you will start to notice it more and more the harder you work to ignore that curiosity.

We were born with it. As children growing up, we constantly asked questions. Why is the sky blue? Why is the grass green? Why, why, why? Anyone who has spent time around a toddler has experienced the endless curiosity that they can bring. For some people, having to constantly answer questions can be very exhausting.

I am sure there were moments when my daughter was growing up where I found myself wondering if the questions would ever end, much like I'm sure my mother wondered the same thing as I was growing up.

Openness (Willingness)

For curiosity to be present, a person needs to open themselves up to let it in. If you come from a mindset that you know everything you need to or that there is nothing new worthwhile for you to learn, you become stagnant. Anytime we look to grow or evolve, we must make room for that change to happen.

An important aspect of curiosity is to remember that it may not be about finding the "one" answer. Or at least that it might not be the answer you first thought you would encounter. Sometimes there are multiple answers or ideas to explore—letting go of having that one perfect solution is integral to genuine and powerful curiosity.

Just like ogres and onions have layers, so does curiosity. As I find some new level of awareness, I get curious again and see what's below that. I continue to look one layer deeper, again and again. That has helped to really open me up and look at things in ways that I might not have otherwise.

To be able to dive deeply into curiosity, we need to adopt *shoshin*, also known as a "beginner's mind." It comes from Zen Buddhism and refers to "having an attitude of openness, eagerness, and lack of preconceptions when studying a subject, even when studying at an advanced level, just as a beginner would." (Jeyachandran 2021)

I encountered this concept when I was doing my professional coach training. Initially, I struggled with letting go of the things I already knew, which held me back from getting to that place of deep curiosity. As we gain more experience and become more knowledgeable about a subject, it can get even more difficult to "let go of what you know."

I have learned to recognize that when I start getting curious about something, it means I need to do some deeper digging.

I acknowledge and appreciate that I will never know everything I need to know. I'm okay with that. I consider myself a lifelong learner and always enjoy starting that next endeavor that will help me grow.

My curiosity has become a secret signal that makes me sit up and pay attention.

Finding the Question

Once you have stepped into curiosity with openness, you have to develop some focus on what question you are exploring. Curiosity for its own sake has value, and mining for what the common theme or thread is running throughout can be very powerful in fueling it.

I am known to fall down TED black holes from time to time. I'll start watching a video that someone recommended to me, or simply one that I happened upon. Once that video has finished, before I know it, I'm looking up another one—and then another one.

There have been more than a few times where I start with the intent to watch one video or talk, and an hour or two later, I'm then looking up and realizing how much time has passed. One of those explorations led me to Tony Porter's TED Talk, "A Call to Men."

In it, he describes the "man box," which captures the collective socialization of men:

"Growing up as a boy, we were taught that men had to be tough, had to be strong, had to be courageous, dominating, no pain, no emotions—with the exception of anger—and definitely no fear. That men are in charge, which means women are not; that men lead, and you should just follow and do what we say; that men are superior; women are inferior; that men are strong; women are weak; that women are of less value, property of men, and objects, particularly sexual objects." (Porter 2010)

Tony's talk got me wrapped up in the question of what I had been taught, whether intentionally or not, by some of the male role models I had in my life. I wondered what elements of that "man box" I had allowed to be set as my reality, and why it was chafing the vision of how I wanted to be as a man.

One particular part of the "man box" was the idea that men shouldn't cry or openly express emotions, except for anger. I saw that demonstrated in many of the examples I saw of men in the media and, to a lesser degree, grown men I had interacted with as a child.

As I looked into it over the years, I realized that being with my emotions as well as expressing them (in healthy ways) allowed me to avoid being run by my emotions. I was able to experience them and not wind up hijacked by them.

My parents divorced when I was four years old, and my father wasn't involved in my life. As a result, many of the male role models I saw were on TV or in the media as I was growing up. A few men in my life were role models, though none modeled a sense of masculinity that I attribute to the way a Whole Man would show up. That's not a criticism of those men; I know they were operating from the examples of masculinity they themselves had seen in their lives.

Exploring/Testing Beliefs

The final part about curiosity is being willing to test the beliefs you were holding before. This brings back the idea of a beginner's mind and goes a step further.

In a science experiment, you begin with a hypothesis. You have an idea that you want to challenge or test to see if it is valid or not. You form your hypothesis and begin comparing it to what you see and experience. That testing then results in a confirmation that your hypothesis was valid, or it wasn't.

The same is true when we are applying curiosity. For me, I had a concept of what masculinity represented based on the teachings I had received, my experiences, and the societal norms that had been shared with me. Like many, I had continued to believe that the structure was valid.

Then I got curious.

I adopted a hypothesis: was my current structure and framework around masculinity not inclusive or encompassing enough for me as a man? (And likely for others too?)

I began wondering if those accepted norms were more restrictive than they should be, and if that was causing me to close off parts of myself. I continue to test against that hypothesis and dismantle the old structure that isn't valid for me.

When it comes to curiosity, something to keep in mind is that it may not lead you to a final destination. In some ways, it can be like the rabbit hole that Alice falls into; you keep tumbling further and further, not knowing where it's going to end.

I have found that when I get curious about one thing, it can often branch into other wonderful areas that I might not have originally considered had I not been willing to explore in the first place.

Sometimes while you are exploring, you will be traveling alone. Other times you will meet people along the way. Similar to hiking on a trail, you may encounter people who are heading in a similar direction, though they're not likely going to the exact same destination. There can be safety and companionship in walking a short while with them and sharing conversation until your paths diverge.

Exploring curiosity and testing the beliefs that you held before can benefit from that same connection. One of the often-unexpected delights in this is that they may mention some areas or paths for you to explore that you hadn't considered. You may return the favor and share some areas for them as well where you found some interest.

As you continue exploring, it is important to pause and look back to evaluate the information you have received against your initial hypothesis or the question you began exploring. When you make these stops, you will have gained new information and will be able to evaluate whether the question you began exploring is still the direction to head or whether you need to adjust your course.

There can be many ways to access and discover what question it is that you need to explore further. You could follow a thread or theme of things that draw your attention. Perhaps one question keeps coming up to you repeatedly, in which case, dive deeper.

For some people, it helps to pay attention to what is bothering or frustrating you in your life. Then you look at which of your beliefs or ideas isn't being honored there and explore more about that. Sometimes we need to get clear on what we *don't* want in order to help us better understand what we *do* want.

You may find yourself going down a path exploring one question, and several other branches appear heading off that path. You cannot always know where they will go, and the only way to find out is to begin exploring the ones that call out to you.

Some will wander and meet back with that main path; others will take you far afield. There is never a "right" or "wrong" path to follow when you are exploring curiosity. Each thing you discover along the way gives you more information than you had before and will create new insights for you.

Where you wander—and which path you choose to follow—is less important than the *willingness to explore.*

To find clues as to where to start wandering, just tune in to the world around you. The universe will continue giving you hints and nudging you. You can tune in or ignore those. Just know that the hints will get louder and more frequent if it is something that you should be looking into.

The next time you start getting curious about something, don't let yourself get caught up in judging if it's the right thing to do or the right question to explore. Just take off and remember to keep curious as you go. And if you need to redirect to a new destination, change course.

Here are some questions to help you connect to your curiosity:

- **What is a subject that excites me to think about?**
- **What topic/issue keeps coming to my awareness/ attention?**
- **What idea keeps circling in my mind?**
- **What thing/topic is bothering me? What about it could I explore?**
- **What is that thing that people keep coming to me to talk about?**
- **Where is that area of my life that I've avoided looking at?**

After you have tapped into your curiosity surrounding how you can become a Whole Man, you must develop your awareness. This is the kind of awareness that goes beyond just saying to yourself, "Yeah, I'm pretty squared away; I've got this."

This is about taking a very real and intense look at yourself and where you are at.

It is coming with an open mind and a willingness to let go of whatever preconceived notions you have about who you should be. Sometimes the best way to help you fine-tune your awareness is to get input from an outside source, someone you trust and respect.

CHAPTER 6

AWARENESS

In 2015, I was doing the first of four experiential retreats in the Co-Active Leadership Program. It is a ten-month-long experiential program that helps you "identify and break through self-perceived limits, putting you on the road to a deeper and richer expression of yourself as a leader." [https://coactive.com/training/leadership-training/] One day the program leaders were giving us individual feedback on how we were showing up in a leadership capacity, which included the impact we were creating as a result.

Elaine, one of the leaders, was one of those people who you immediately connect with. She didn't tolerate BS and gave it to you straight. And when she gave it to you, it always came from a place of love and support. Elaine was also insanely good at seeing through you and speaking the truth you needed to hear, even when you didn't necessarily want to hear it.

We were participating in an activity, and as I approached her, she said, "You are really good at connecting with people, I can tell. It's something that comes naturally for you." I smiled and nodded as I felt this was indeed something that was a strength for me.

Then she dropped the truth bomb on me.

"But you don't stay and let them connect deeply with you in return. You don't let them in, instead keeping them at arm's length."

Shit.

If I was in a movie, this would be where the suspenseful music gets cued, and the camera starts to swirl around as though there's confusion and chaos happening. I was turned completely upside down and inside out.

She was absolutely right. And it really hurt to realize she knew what I'd been trying to hide all this time.

Those few short sentences she spoke sliced right to my core.

A part of me knew that one of the ways I protected myself was to keep people at arm's distance, yet I didn't admit that to myself. Her speaking those words out loud meant that I could not ignore it anymore, that it jumped front and center into my awareness. I also knew in that moment that I couldn't keep avoiding it, even though it was a little intimidating to consider opening myself up like that.

Now that I was aware of what I had been avoiding, I was able to start digging into it and seeing where it needed to lead me. While I initially resisted, it turned out to be one of the most amazing gifts I could have received.

That experience opened me up to the awareness that I needed to make a change, and before I could begin to make headway on growing, I needed to take time to establish a foundation and recognize where I was beginning the journey from.

Establish the Baseline

When I was in Marine Officer Candidates School, we learned how to navigate with a map and compass so that we could find our way to the mission objective. To have any chance of success in that, you had to have a clear idea of where you started. Having a destination does you no good at all if you don't understand where you are starting from. Awareness is no different, except instead of navigating through terrain, we're navigating in our own lives as we find our way.

Awareness breaks down into two main areas:

- Who you are.
- Where you need to grow.

It begins with taking the time to understand who you are as a person. What makes you tick? Just like the example of navigating with a map, how can you really know who you are if you don't know where you are starting from?

Here are some questions you might pull from as you are looking to understand your starting point. There are many different ways to begin, so feel free to create your own questions as well.

- What are my natural strengths or talents?
- How well do I use them?
- Are there any I'm overusing? If so, how?
- What do I do well?
- What is harder for me to do?
- What potential blind spots or areas for improvement do I have?
- What skills or talents do I need to develop?

Ultimately, we are products of all the experiences to this point in our lives. We have our cores of who we are, and many other external influences will also shape that—your family dynamics growing up, culture and religion, economic factors. The list goes on and on.

This is not about to become a dissertation on the development of the psyche and our personalities. Other people are much better suited to talk about that than I am. What I do want to point out is that many things influence who we are. Very often, those things may not seem obvious to us.

Much like the story of the frog in the pot of boiling water, when we have these small, recurring influences on a regular basis, we may not always see how much they shape how we have developed and who we have become. Sometimes we need an outside source to help bring our attention to what we might be overlooking (or likely ignoring) about our own behaviors.

As humans, we are not always as effective as we could be around honestly evaluating ourselves. We tend to be critical of others and more forgiving of our own flaws along the way. We like to pay attention to the parts of ourselves that we believe are good and downplay the ones that might not be as positive, or the ones that might be less socially acceptable by the masses.

Think of the last time you did an assessment. You may have told yourself at the beginning that you were going to be very honest in your responses so that you could get the best possible results. If you're like most people, chances are that somewhere along the way, how you answered some of the questions may have shifted slightly.

Perhaps it was a question that you looked at and thought, "Well, I'm not completely like that, but I'm working toward it, and I'm sure that's how I'd really show up." So, you begin to answer more in alignment with who you want to be or who you see yourself as, instead of who you might truly be showing up as on a day-to-day basis.

I am a big fan of assessments, and I frequently use them with my clients. I have also learned that they are just information. An assessment is simply a tool. Using the right tool at the right time can be very effective and powerful.

The potential pitfall comes in when we involve the human factor. I may have the best intentions when I start out an assessment that I want to answer truthfully. And, like many others, I know sometimes I paint myself in a better light.

Where assessments can really shine is if you start to see similar results coming from multiple areas of your life. That can start to point you to an area that you need to work on or pay some attention to. For those familiar with 360 assessments, you can compile input from a number of people that can paint a more complete (though not absolute) picture of how you show up and interact with others. While practical in some instances, they're not useful everywhere.

Where you aren't able to effectively use one, you can begin to notice the feedback you get from others. Is there a common theme they point to? Is there a particular thing you do well that they often call upon you for? Is there something you're capable of, yet others don't reach out to you to do? These can all be information you use as you evaluate where you are and want to go or grow.

One common theme I've found across the years and the various assessments I've done is that I love to begin new endeavors. The creative process really lights me up. Where I don't have a natural strength is in the ongoing minutiae and seeing things through to completion. I am often prone to "ooh, squirrel!" moments. Knowing this about myself, I have to consciously focus on driving certain undertakings to completion or making a choice to build a team to help with it.

In this case, it was the repeated and similar feedback I got from the assessments that have helped me recognize this area for myself and not let it become something that holds me back, as it would if I had ignored it.

One other way that we can help establish our baseline is by getting input from people we know and trust. Getting feedback from people who see us from the outside can provide invaluable insight. Just like the example that I shared at the beginning of this chapter, Elaine did that for me.

When you ask others for this feedback, being clear and specific on what feedback you want is important. That helps make it easier for them to pay attention to the particular area where you want to expand your own awareness and prevents them from giving vague or unhelpful feedback that doesn't serve. In much of the training I facilitate, I encourage participants to seek feedback as part of their learning.

Asking for specific and quantifiable feedback is good, and you should also be open to spontaneous feedback too. This can be a great barometer of our impact when we're not consciously focused on it because we know we're being evaluated.

In choosing people to give you feedback, selecting people who know you in different aspects of your life can be useful. Some may be family friends; others might be coworkers or colleagues. Each will have seen you in a different light and in a different setting, which will give you richer information. Be conscious of whom you select based upon where you want to grow awareness.

Standing in front of the mirror and really looking at who you are and being honest about what you see takes courage.

You have to be able to look at the light and the shadow—the strengths and the weaknesses. This means you need to step into real honesty and clarity about yourself, or you won't be able to understand where you need to grow to become a Whole Man.

I had to stop and take stock in the fact that I kept people at arm's length for much of my life, and as a result, it kept me from the deeper connection I was truly craving. When I was able to own that and face it, it allowed me to shift and transform.

Knowing Where to Go

After you have taken the time to get clear on where you are, then you can begin to look at where you need to go and where you want to grow. Determining that version of yourself that you aspire to grow into or having an idea of the goal you want to work toward will help you map out the path to get there.

Having specific goals is sometimes important. Goals tend to be specific and measurable so you can evaluate your progress toward accomplishing them. When it comes to personal growth, those goals you are seeking may not be as easily quantifiable. In these cases, it is more of a direction you are moving toward than it is a specific destination you are aiming for.

Wandering can provide great value at times in your life. On a couple of occasions, I have ventured out toward something, not fully sure of what it would look like when I got there, yet aware I was being called or pulled somewhere. I knew moving away from where I was would serve me far better than simply standing still.

At some point in the wandering, a greater clarity came along and helped me define where my destination was. Being open to new information and opportunities along the way is helpful, or else you will never make meaningful progress.

For me, an example of this has shown up in a couple of ways. First, this very book you are reading! When I started exploring vulnerability for myself as a man, it led me to start talking with other men about the topic. That evolved into a podcast, and now this book. If I had waited back at the starting point to try and figure out every twist and turn, this might not have come to be. Different things begin to show up once you start along your path—things you couldn't see from where you were, which only become visible as you make progress.

The Whole Man understands the value of continually bettering himself. He has a willingness to continue learning, not just about himself but also about how he relates and interacts with other people. He keeps on the lookout for where old ways of being and old ideas of how the world is may be holding him back.

Just like computers, we have operating systems running in ourselves continually. These are built on our past experiences and encounters with people and shape the way we act in different situations. The danger in continuing to let them run unattended is that they may be working off outdated information that will not allow us to move forward.

Masculine and Feminine Energy

One such area that needs to be explored is where we need to pull apart the idea of masculinity and femininity from the concept of masculine and feminine energy. We have constructed the idea that masculine energy belongs to men and that feminine energy belongs to women.

That cannot be further from the truth.

We all have access to both, yet often we are not made aware of that. If a man demonstrates some of the traits that are often associated with feminine energy, he tends to get labeled as being "unmanly."

Alexandra Tiodar's article "The Truth About Masculine and Feminine Energy Explained" outlines some of the traits often associated with the Divine Masculine and Divine Feminine: (Tiodar 2021).

Divine Masculine	Divine Feminine
Taking action	Gentleness
Assertiveness	Kindness
Physical force	Heart-centeredness
Decision-making	Creativity
Leadership	Intuition
Protection	Acceptance
Logical thinking and reasoning	Receiving
Achieving	Emotionality
Being goal-oriented	Communication
Providing	Compassion
	Empathy
	Understanding
	Forgiveness

Suppose you're like me (and, quite frankly, many other people), you may identify with traits from both sides of these lists. I also see that in some messaging I received as a young boy, some of the traits or characteristics listed on the right were not as readily encouraged or expected of me—at least from some of the boys or men that I interacted with.

I was raised by a single mother, and she often demonstrated characteristics from both sides of these lists. I personally believe there are masculine energies and traits, as well as feminine energies and traits; however, no one is 100 percent on either side. We have a bit of both. I don't see it as a polarity of people being either male or female. Men could have mostly feminine traits and still be men, and vice versa.

As a result, I knew I could access the energies that are often associated with the divine feminine, yet I didn't always advertise that. I became very conscious about when and where I chose to do that. I share this because part of my awareness on my journey around where I needed to grow was to show those characteristics more often and do so without attachment to how other men would receive them.

One of the ways this would show up is in hiding or suppressing my emotions and feelings. I would downplay how I felt unless it was certain emotions. I knew I was in touch with my feelings but didn't always broadcast that to others. If I showed emotions, I was conscious of which men were around when I did it.

For a good portion of my life, I followed in line with the other examples I saw at the time. Making sure that I was displaying the "right" type of energy that I should as a man and being very selective about where I might talk about or openly express the connection I had to that feminine energy.

I came to understand that in the military or in construction, there wasn't openness in talking about a version of masculinity other than what this stereotype of those careers portrayed. These were very hypermasculine spaces, and to show up otherwise, you risked becoming an outcast. A type of masculinity helps men be successful in these (and other) fields, and I believe there's room for expanding the success factors too.

As I continue to grow my awareness of how I view masculinity, I recognize that I need to keep exploring how I see the concept of masculine and feminine energy—how they impact me as a man and impact the way that I behave and show up in my relationships with the people in my world. There's value for all men in looking at this element of masculinity, as well as which areas each man needs to explore further for himself.

Checking In

In sailing, you may recognize that sailboats rarely move in a straight line toward their destination. They tack back and forth, zigzagging to catch the wind and keep momentum. The ship's captain continually adjusts based on the conditions and their progress, evaluating where they are against where they want to get to.

The same idea applies as you continue expanding your awareness. You need to assess where you currently are in relation to where you want to go.

When I was a construction project manager, we used milestones to help us determine how we were doing in making progress toward our project deadlines. The various teams would gather on a regular basis and check in with each other to see how their respective parts were doing, alongside the progress of the collective project. This was a way we measured progress against the desired end result.

Whether you are referencing the baseline you left from or the destination you are heading to you, you will need to check in from time to time. You gain information in everything that you do and then use that information to gauge how much progress you have made and where you need to shift.

Analyzing each step you take to see what the impact is and what ramifications it has on your chosen path is part of the process. With each step, each move, you gain new information that you didn't have before. You then apply that new information against your goal and adjust as needed or continue on the same path.

The same applies as you are looking to grow your awareness. From time to time, you will check back and look at where your curiosity originally pointed you. You'll consider the spaces you have explored, and where you are currently.

Be cautious not to let yourself fall into the trap of gauging how fast or slow you should be moving. The danger of comparing ourselves to others is seductive, especially when it comes to progress.

Plato once said, "Never discourage anyone who continually makes progress, no matter how slow." We are each on our own journey, and none but ourselves can determine the rate at which we advance. A good friend of mine often says, "Progress, not perfection," as a way to remind herself that moving and momentum are far more important than getting it perfect.

Know that at times you will feel like you are going backward. Sometimes when we explore new territory, we have to retrace our steps as we check in. Not every path leads where we expect, and we only discover that after wandering down it a little.

You may need to find some places you don't want to go before you get more clarity on where you do. If this happens, be patient with yourself.

I have no desire to run a marathon. Frankly, I stopped running when the Marine Corps stopped paying me to run. I have friends who run marathons and ultramarathons, and they have shared with me that one of the ways they help track how they're doing is by looking at their split times for each mile. It allows them to look at an individual mile—or even the last several miles—and then they determine what adjustments they need to make in order to keep on their desired pace.

You will not be able to set a stopwatch to track each milestone you hit as you continue your journey to becoming a Whole Man. Each of us will move at different speeds. You may not be able to measure progress quantifiably, and you will start to notice a qualitative shift in how you show up and who you are being.

Let *that* be the yardstick you measure with. Make sure you are noticing the input you are getting from other people around you. They may start commenting on how you are being different, and that can be another way to help you check in and see how you are doing with your progress.

Remember, awareness can be boiled down to the ideas of: "Who are you?" and "Where do you need to grow?" These ideas revolve around the premise that you are ultimately in charge and that you are the one guiding the journey.

You **establish your baseline** and begin with getting clear on where you are. This can come from introspection, assessments, external feedback, or some combination of all of these.

You **determine where you want to go** by setting goals or sometimes beginning to wander until the goals become clear.

You **check in** to evaluate your progress toward that destination or goal and make adjustments with the new information you gain along the way.

In the next chapter, we will explore presence, which is the third habit of the Whole Man.

CHAPTER 7

PRESENCE

———

In our hectic and non-stop world, we are often pulled from whatever we are currently doing toward whatever the next thing is that we're supposed to be doing. We are bombarded by stimulus and noise, constantly scrambling to get our attention. We have access to the internet and information in a way today that was not possible even twenty or thirty years ago.

Just the other day, I was driving in the car with my daughter. Out of the blue, she asked me if I knew what the average height was for men around the world. I told her I had no idea. She pulled out her phone, started searching, and for the next few minutes, regaled me with the average height of men and women worldwide and through various countries in the world.

It made me marvel at how much things had changed. As a kid, if I had wondered the same question, I would have had to go to the library and find an encyclopedia. (For those who have no idea what that is, it was often a set of books that had a ton of information on many different subjects.) Yes, I recognize that some who read this never existed in a world where information wasn't readily available via smartphone or computer.

Don't get me wrong; I am a big fan of technology. It has enabled us to do so much more than we could have even a generation ago. My smartphone has more capability than my very first Commodore 64 computer from when I was a kid. (Yes, I'm old enough that that was my first computer; stop laughing.) Phones today have more computing ability than the first supercomputer that was built decades ago.

These advances in technology are also a double-edged sword. They allow us to do so much more, and as a result, we are expected to do more.

The constant battle for our attention often keeps us with our heads down and continually driving forward, preventing us from slowing down and pausing—simply taking a breath. We rarely take time to really connect with the current moment, as opposed to what happened an hour or a day ago, or what we must get done later today or tomorrow, or next week. We feel like there is too much to do and not enough time.

Quick Tip: The next time you're feeling a little (or a lot) overwhelmed with things, put your device down, or turn away from that computer screen. Take thirty seconds and just tune into your breathing. Let your body settle for a moment. Take a few deep breaths, and then return to what you were doing. While it might not seem like much, even that short pause will make a difference. (And it turns out the world didn't implode because you didn't send that email or send that text!)

We are in a state in our world where not only do we expect instant gratification, but it also creates stress for us if we don't get instant responses to our text and email messages. Think about the last time you sent a text message to someone when you needed a response quickly. When they didn't respond immediately, how did that feel? You might have thought,

"Don't they understand that I need this information right now? Wasn't it obvious?"

Now think about a time when someone has sent you a message and then followed it up with another message looking for a response moments later. You probably thought they were being needy or that they were not being considerate of the fact that you might need some time to get back to them. Maybe you were busy doing something and couldn't reply immediately. What a crazy concept, right?

Funny how we don't always offer that same perspective when we are the ones needing the information.

Consciously Choose

For a good part of my life, I believed that presence was just about where my physical body was located. I never gave much thought to how it impacted things around me based on where my attention was. After my daughter was born, that changed. I became acutely aware of tuning in to each moment when I was with her, which also began to extend into my interactions with other people in my life.

Presence begins with a conscious choice to slow down and connect to *this* moment.

It requires us to notice when we're caught up in the whirlwind of everything going on and then choose to stop.

This also builds upon awareness from the previous habit of the Whole Man. We need to be honest with ourselves about our priorities and how much time and effort we are directing to things that aren't really a priority for us. Most often, we let others set our priorities, which leaves us frustrated or burnt out.

Choosing to make yourself a priority is equally important. It's also one of the things most of us (myself included) don't do as often as we should.

Build Your Boundaries

To combat our "always-on" culture, we need to find ways to create more presence in our lives. It requires muting or tuning out the external noise that clamors for your attention and just connecting with yourself. It is different from ignoring or avoiding, and we need to have a level of self-discipline to do this well.

Our world and the people in it will continually make demands of your time, energy, and attention. For some people, it is hard to say no when people make requests, and that is where building boundaries will help.

To build boundaries, you need to understand and manage the expectations you are willing to let others place upon you. It also means you need to get clear about your expectations of others.

The most powerful word I have learned that has enabled me to set and maintain boundaries is "no."

We understand what the word means, yet we use it with hesitancy, or we don't use it in the moments we should.

That friend who sends you a text message asking if you have five minutes to talk when you know it will wind up taking twenty minutes or more. The colleague who once again asks you to help them out with something as they promise this will be the last time, and that they will return the favor very soon (even though it has never happened).

Right now, you have someone in your life you have trouble saying no to. Don't worry; I'm not going to reveal your secret.

We were brought up to think that being polite also carries an expectation of saying yes when people ask for help. Assisting others is important, but we aren't taught that saying no is okay sometimes, especially when saying yes can have a detrimental impact on us.

Building boundaries will create great leverage and allow us to be more present in two primary areas:

- Time
- Attention

Time

Unless you have discovered something the rest of us don't know, you only have twenty-four hours in your day. That time is our most precious non-renewable resource, and so many of us waste it without a second thought. (Okay, I own that was a little punny now that I read it, and I'm okay with that.)

I start with time because if you become capable of building and maintaining boundaries around your time, it will make the other areas much easier to handle. When you're looking at building boundaries around time, it is important to start small in your thinking. Look for ways that you can start to find small chunks of time to claim back instead of looking for hours at a time. The number of ways you can apply this or the different areas you can look at is only bound by your imagination.

Some days I am stupefied by the volume of emails I receive. I used to be of the mindset that when one came in, I had to respond immediately or at least in very short order. I became good at replying in a short amount of time and recognized that it was significantly impacting the quality and quantity of work I was doing in other areas.

I would be in the middle of doing something that had all my attention, and the notification would pop up for an email. I would stop what I was doing, click on the notification, figure out what I needed to say or do in order to respond, and then go back to what I had been doing before the email came in.

I told myself I'd just respond to "that one email." Usually, I'd reply to that one and then notice one or two more I could just take care of quickly as well "since I'm already in my inbox."

Several minutes later (okay, maybe twenty minutes), I finally pull myself out of my emails to get back to what I was doing. But now, I need some time to reconnect with it and get back into the zone.

That "one" email resulted in a lot of lost productivity and time (not to mention that my inner critic would now have plenty of ammunition for beating me up for the lost time and progress… oy vey!).

In my mind, I was being efficient and responsive, and I continued operating under that false pretense until I met Dave Crenshaw at a conference. He had just published his book, *The Myth of Multitasking*, and had spoken at a breakout about his idea of multitasking and how it keeps us from performing anywhere near our optimal levels. He coined the term "switchtasking" as:

Switchtasking = attempting to do multiple attention-requiring tasks at the same time. Each switch in attention incurs switching cost, which includes a loss of time, a decrease in performance, and an increase in stress levels. When most people say they are "multitasking," they are most often referring to switchtasking. (Davecrenshaw.com)

As much as I didn't want to believe it and was convinced I was great at switchtasking, the fact was his research (and my own experiences) proved otherwise.

One of the biggest gifts that came from that experience was that I started building time into each of my days where I would respond to emails. At first, it was challenging, but I found that setting aside a couple of blocks of time during the day to respond to messages allowed me to be responsive enough to people and still have focused time for me to get work done.

Attention

The other area where I began creating boundaries was around attention—where my attention was when I was in different situations, and which people I was giving attention to. As I continued gaining more time and productivity back from the boundaries I kept, it brought my awareness to some of the people I was giving time and attention to.

I started evaluating if I was spending that most precious resource on people who might not have deserved it or who did not deserve as much as I was giving them.

I began paying more attention to being fully present in conversations I was having. If I was in a meeting in my office, I would lock my computer or turn off my monitor so that it wouldn't be a distraction. If I was in a meeting in someone else's office, I would put my phone on silent so that I would not be distracted by notifications.

I became more aware of the people who I was letting fill up my calendar with meetings I really didn't need to attend or conversations that could be handled in an email instead. I became more ruthless around where I was letting others pull my attention, and I got better at focusing that attention where I needed to have it.

A couple of ways I was able to implement this:

- When someone would invite me to a meeting I likely didn't need to attend, I would call them to ask what they needed from me for the meeting, or why they felt I should be there. More often than not, I received a response like, "Just figured you should be in the know." I was able to arrange with some that they would simply forward me any key meeting points afterward.
- Standing meetings: for some of our weekly team check-in meetings, I made them fifteen-minute standing meetings instead. It allowed us to get to the point and share what needed to be shared instead of simply filling time.
- I started paying more attention to meetings I was scheduling that might not have been needed. Additionally, I began scheduling fifteen-minute meetings instead of thirty-minute ones. This forced me to get to the point, and it turns out other people appreciated the shorter meetings!

Building boundaries and saying no to people who want our attention will not always be easy. This again comes back to having some awareness of the people you should be giving less of your time to.

One way I began sorting through people was by looking at my interactions with them. I tuned in to whether my interactions with certain people left me more energized or more drained after having contact with them. I also looked beyond one encounter; I evaluated it over a span of time.

For the ones who tended to drain my energy or left me feeling worse off than before I spent time with them, it helped me realize I wanted to give them less of my time. For the people who boosted my energy, I chose to make more time available to them. The hidden gift in this was that I was enjoying the people I engaged with more, and it had me feeling more active and excited about things.

Sometimes you may make concessions and let those boundaries slip a little. In the long run, the more clearly you establish the boundaries, the easier it will be to say no to things that will cross them. This will allow you to say yes to the things that you want and need to be doing in your life. Best of all, you will be more present in those moments as well.

Unplug (or Technology Detox)

I remember growing up as a kid when my mom and I would have game nights. We would pull out a board game or a deck of cards and just spend hours lost in the play, enjoying each other's company and the connection of the moment. There was great conversation, lots of laughs, and a ton of memories that will be with me forever. I recognize this was a time before cellphones were common, and what I cherished most about these memories is how connected and present we were in those moments.

Social media was designed to create more connections and bring us together.

The irony is that when people connect through the likes of Facebook, Instagram, or other platforms, that connection is at arm's length. It is a curated and closed-off connection that we tell ourselves represents reality, yet it is simply the form of reality we choose to let our world see.

It is one of the most dangerous types of marketing because we see it and believe it's real and then begin to question why we don't have all our shit together like the people we're following.

I believe this constant need for connection in our always-connected world is creating barriers to real and deep connection.

Try this out… the next time you walk down the street or are out in public, put your phone away. Take a moment and look around. So many people nowadays move with their faces in their electronic devices, oblivious to the world around them.

I have lost track of the number of times I have seen people walk into things because they are distracted by their devices. (I will admit—and I realize this may make me sound a little twisted—I laugh a little bit when I see somebody walk into something because they're so absorbed in their device. If that makes me a bad person, oh well, I can live with it.)

While we're on the subject of distraction, don't even get me started about people driving and looking at their phones as well. I have stopped counting the number of times people have almost run into me or swerved into my lane, and I see them looking at their phones while driving. Or people sitting there after the light has turned green because they've been sucked into their phones.

Unplugging from our devices from time to time is crucial for being deeply present. This means putting away our phones, turning off the TV, and shutting down our computers so we can slow down and be present.

Some of you read that last sentence and started breaking out in a cold sweat at the thought of not having your devices at your fingertips. Don't worry. I'm not asking you to quit altogether. I am asking you to find moments where you can disconnect from the matrix and be in your reality.

We used to have what I called "Tech-free Tuesdays" in our house. After I got home from work and we had finished dinner, we would put devices away and just spend quality time as a family. Sometimes we would play games or cards; other times, we would all get a book and just sit together reading in the same space, with conversations sprinkled throughout.

We would take turns on who got to decide what we would be doing that evening, which kept us engaged and allowed everyone to have a chance at doing something they really enjoyed. The card game Uno quickly became one of my daughter's favorites because she enjoyed playing "Draw Two" and "Wild Draw Four" cards on me. I might have hammed it up a little when she did, and if so, it was because I enjoyed the playful banter it created between us.

Just like things like this were an opportunity to create great memories for me as a kid, I know it did the same for my daughter.

Being present is a muscle that we typically aren't taught how to use, and as a result, it feels awkward for us when we begin practicing it. By the same token, if we don't use that muscle, it will atrophy and wither, making it all the harder to start using again. For anyone who has exercised, those unused or under-utilized muscles may hurt a little when you start using them, and over time they get stronger and easier to use.

We need to exercise this muscle more.

We have lots of examples telling us to look back at experiences or look forward and "keep your eyes on the prize" so we know what goals we're after. There is value in learning from experiences and setting goals, but we need to be cautious about staring for too long.

One of the unique things about our human experience is that we are only capable of existing in *this very moment*, even while our minds can think forward and backward through time. This becomes a trap when we dwell on something for too long. We sit and daydream and plan about all the wonderful things that will happen when we accomplish our goals, lose that weight, or land that amazing job.

The Whole Man invests time in building the capacity to be present. He recognizes the value in doing so, consciously chooses to make it a practice, builds the boundaries he needs, and knows when and how to unplug so he can connect in the moment with the people he needs to.

Here's an exercise I discovered in my coach training that I do from time to time when I find myself distracted and not present. It helps me slow down and get grounded:

- I settle into my chair or seat, lean back, and relax my body.
- I take a few deep breaths, inhaling and exhaling slowly.
- I reflect for a few moments, "What was I doing one year ago today?" and see where my mind goes. Then I reflect on "What will I be doing one year from today?"
- Then, "What was I doing one month ago?" "What will I be doing one month from now?"
- I ask the same questions of:
  - One hour ago / one hour from now.
  - One minute ago / one minute from now.
  - One second ago / one second from now.
- Then I tune into what is here in this moment right now—and in this moment… and in this moment.

In the next chapter, we are going to explore the habit of emotional health. Buckle up!

CHAPTER 8

EMOTIONAL HEALTH

In July 2021, I interviewed Jordan Holmes on *The Vulnerable Man* podcast, and as we were talking about therapy and his #howmencry project, he had this to share (Veal 2021):

> The project #howmencry is looking to do two things. One is to make showing vulnerability a norm amongst men, and two is to help to normalize the conversations around mental health and hopefully help to point men toward therapy and support services. The way that I landed on that project was really just a process of kind of going through mental breakdown. Basically, I was at a point of being very, very stressed from chasing a lot of the different hats that I wear.
>
> I was kind of pushing those things forward so much, and wasn't really resolving or looking to what was happening to me as a person really. And I just—I got to a point of burnout. I just felt like I was kind of at this snapping point. And the woman I was dating at the time, just from the different hardships that were going into our relationship, was really suggesting that

I went to therapy and find some help, just from some
of the things that I dealt with, within my childhood.
And, you know, she was—she was correct in the need
to do so.

And I basically said to her, if—you know—you go
and find a therapist, I'll go. And she did; so I went.
And, you know, it seemed that seems a lot more simple than with that process actually was right. You
know, but I went and just really started to dig into a
lot of those earlier childhood things that really—that
really carried a lot of influence into what my actions
were today.

I've struggled with depression, suicidal thoughts,
you name it, as far as the depths that I've been through
at different points of my life. And to be honest, if I was
at a point that I felt like I was snapping—I felt like I
couldn't take it anymore is literally the best way that
I could describe it. So, in my deepest point I felt like
I have to do something different or things will melt
down. I just didn't have any other way to go or at least
it felt that way. And it was honestly pretty much the
best decision I've made in my in my adult life.

Take a walk through your local bookstore or convenience
store, and you'll see dozens of magazines committed to physical health and fitness. Probably twice as many are dedicated
to fashion and makeup. How many will you find that talk
about emotional health and wellness?

My guess is zero.

Companies spend billions of dollars each year bombard-
ing us with messages telling us how we should look, what
we should wear, and what we should do with our lives and

our free time. They put blinders on us, wanting us to focus on how we look and appear to others—while stepping over how we feel inside.

We are experiencing an emotional health crisis in our world, and the pandemic is only worsening the situation. According to a study published by the Boston University School of Public Health, "Depression among adults in the United States tripled in the early 2020 months of the global coronavirus pandemic—jumping from 8.5 percent before the pandemic to a staggering 27.8 percent. That rate has continued to rise, and in 2021 affects nearly 1 in every 3 American adults." (McKoy 2020)

Moreover, in the United States in 2019 (American Foundation for Suicide Prevention 2019):

- Suicide was the tenth leading cause of death.
- 90% of those who died by suicide had a diagnosable mental health condition at the time of their death.
- 10.3% of Americans have thought about suicide, and
- 54% of Americans have been affected by suicide.

That is unacceptable, and it needs to change. When I see those statistics, I almost don't believe them. While I've never struggled with suicidal thoughts, I know I've had points where I have felt down or depressed. What shocked me the most is that more than half of Americans have been affected by suicide. Additionally, so many of those who have died by suicide had a diagnosable mental health condition.

Additionally, per the statistics, men were *nearly four times* more like to die by suicide. This saddens me even more because I know men are rarely willing to talk about the things they are struggling with. I understand how tragic suicide is and didn't realize how mental health played such a heavy factor.

We need to normalize these conversations around mental health and get rid of the stigma surrounding mental health conditions.

Healthy masculinity allows men to come from a place of knowing that asking for help isn't a sign of weakness, that it is instead a show of strength.

Expand Your Emotional Range

Just like young children often don't have a filter for their emotions, at some point they are then told to stifle those feelings. Helping children learn to recognize and process the flood of emotions they experience is important.

As a parent, I remember times when my daughter might have a meltdown as she was feeling overwhelmed by her emotions. She was learning how to be with her emotions, and as parents, we were trying to learn how to support that. I know now that when I see a parent trying to deal with a toddler having a tantrum in the middle of the grocery store, I have a lot more empathy for what they are going through.

At our core, humans are emotional creatures. We all experience emotions; it is part of the human condition. How we are instructed to deal with said emotions is key.

Michael Kaufman says:

"From an early age we bathe boys in notions about a masculinity that requires the suppression of a range of feelings and human possibilities. At a certain age, we require that boys set up emotional boundaries from their friends. Almost from the start, we saw that the tasks of nurturing and caregiving are not for them." (Kaufman 2014).

The unintended impact of these types of messages is that, for boys, certain emotions aren't okay to show, and if you have them, you'd better get over them quickly.

This is not to say that you should let every emotion be expressed in every instant it is felt. Sometimes it may be inappropriate to show the anger or frustration you're feeling.

If I'm at work and a coworker does something that upsets me, it may not be appropriate for me to vent at that moment. I might need to focus on the work at hand and wait to process those emotions at another time. If a doctor feels frustrated with what a patient is saying, they need to be able to put that aside and focus on providing care for the person.

What I'm trying to point out is that men often get told they need to stifle most (if not all) emotions all the time.

This is what trips us up and creates larger problems down the road.

Suppressing or avoiding sets us up only for future problems. I had a client who wanted to work on his stress response in some work settings. He would get triggered and angry about things and would just push that anger down until it would eventually explode, and he would yell at his team during meetings. Because he kept letting it build without processing the emotions, he finally erupted one day in a way that significantly impacted his professional career standing.

He had been told as a boy that he shouldn't let others see him angry, and as a result, he never learned how to find healthy ways to process that anger. It wound up costing him his job.

Emotions are neither good nor bad. They are simply emotions.

I said this back in an earlier chapter, and it bears repeating.

The way to prevent suppressing emotions is to learn how to be with them and process them in a healthy way. When we can experience our emotions, they tend to move through us more readily, and we do not become run by them or held hostage by them.

Fear is something that used to hold me back quite often from taking action, especially in instances where I was up to big goals that were important to me. The way I began dealing with it was by noticing when the fear would come up. When I noticed it, instead of hiding from it or ignoring it, I began to look at what was triggering the fear. As I began looking at it more, it helped me recognize what things were concerns and what were just worries I was emphasizing in my mind.

The more I practiced exploring and unpacking that fear, the less control it had over me, and the more I was able to manage it. It freed me from being a victim of my fear.

The sooner we begin normalizing dealing with emotions, the sooner we can start shifting the dialogue in a healthier direction.

Connect Talking Circles

One resource I have heard men use to connect that has been helpful for them is the concept of men's circles or talking circles. While they have different formats or agendas, one common thread among them is that they seek to create a safe or brave space for men to sit and gather and share or talk about whatever they need to.

Talking circles do not typically come from a mindset or an approach of trying to fix or solve the challenges men bring to the circle. Instead, they simply hold space for hearing what those men have to share.

Some of the men I talked to who have participated in these circles have said that one of the biggest benefits they get, besides the camaraderie of being with other men in that space, is that they often hear other men talk about things and share struggles that are similar to ones they are also having.

That shared experience creates a closeness and a bond, and often opens a willingness in the men to be more open in themselves.

Another powerful (and often overlooked) resource for supporting men's emotional health is therapy.

For many years, the idea of going to therapy was something that seemed acceptable for women only. If you found a man in a therapist's office, he was likely there for marriage or relationship counseling. Much stigma was attached to men even discussing the idea of going to therapy, and I believe that prevented men from seeking help when they were struggling.

In my experience, men are very unlikely to talk about or seek out therapy. Particularly early in my professional life and because of the groups of men I worked with, therapy was a taboo subject.

Since I found my way into coaching and organizational development work, I am finding more men open to talking about it and sharing their experiences of doing therapy. This gives me hope.

Recently that trend has started shifting as we broaden the conversation around mental health and wellness. Hearing men share about having seen a therapist (or that they are currently seeing a therapist) is more common than was the case even just a decade ago. This is a shift in the right direction for sure, and there are still a lot of men who either want to seek therapy or are in therapy yet won't talk about it openly.

Many people fall into the trap of venting to friends all the time. In the short term, it feels good and may help you feel better, yet over the long run, those friends rarely are able to offer the sort of support or help that is truly needed. Our friends, while well-meaning, are only colluding to keep us in unhealthy cycles and not moving toward real help and healing.

I never hesitate to share that I went to therapy in the past. I had a lot going on that I was having difficulty managing and realized that friends who meant well couldn't help me in the way I needed.

I got to a point where I recognized that I was just feeling overwhelmed and starting to detach and isolate myself. I chose to take advantage of my employer's Employee Assistance Program, which included access to counseling and therapy as a benefit.

I know I felt a little uncomfortable making that initial call to get the names of therapists to investigate—but more importantly, I knew I needed it to help me move forward as I was unable to on my own.

Therapy was a godsend.

One of the biggest benefits I received was having an outside voice who wasn't invested or tied up in the situations I was dealing with and could give me an objective perspective on things. Most often, my therapist would just listen and let me process.

One of the key takeaways from the "Care Leads to Care" study is:

"Many men feel tremendous expectation to adhere to stereotypical masculine ideals. Stereotypical masculine norms—in addition to time demands, economic constraints, and cultural expectations around asking for help—combine to create particularly strong obstacles for men to be able to care for themselves the way they would like to." (Gupta 2021)

As you're reading this, if you are undecided on whether to give it a try, please know that I am saying with confidence that yes, you should.

Whether it is through therapy, a men's circle, or simply reaching out to a friend to say that you are experiencing difficulty or struggling, I appreciate that more men today are willing to speak about this topic and, more importantly, are willing to ask for help.

Many men still feel like there is a stigma around the idea of them being in therapy. It may take a while for that perspective to shift, but we are making progress. I know that the more men talk about this and the more we bring it into common discussions, the greater the likelihood that we help men feel safe in sharing they are struggling and need help.

We need to help them understand that asking for help and recognizing that you need it is something that "real men" do.

The Whole Man Approach

The Whole Man recognizes that he can't do it all alone—that there is power in the "we" and that community can help support him when he feels he can't go on. We will all have moments where we are struggling and find life hard to manage. When that happens, we need to admit that we can't do it all on our own and then have the courage to ask for help.

The Whole Man recognizes the importance of maintaining emotional health along with physical health. He makes time to nurture his body so it can sustain him, and he prioritizes time for self-care and emotional health.

He knows that to sustain his emotional health, he needs to expand his emotional range, practice compassion, and connect.

Practicing compassion shows up in two distinct ways: The first, compassion for others, is one that a lot of men are open to doing. Self-compassion, which is the second… well, we tend to struggle with that. Both are necessary to become a Whole Man.

Compassion relates to understanding another person's pain along with a desire to mitigate it. This is different from empathy which is about one's ability to relate to someone's pain vicariously, as if you had experienced it yourself. Compassion does not require empathy; you do not need to have felt similar pain or suffering in order to hold compassion for someone.

At its core, I believe compassion comes down to seeing the humanity in one another and within ourselves. It also includes a willingness to forgive. We are likely to find forgiveness for others when they fail or fall short of our expectations, yet we do not give that same grace to ourselves when we fail.

Of the men I interviewed over the years, the ones who have higher self-compassion tend to have greater comfort with being vulnerable.

Even before the pandemic hit, many organizations had a culture that created pride around overwork and burnout, as if you would earn some unseen badge of honor for going above and beyond or stretching yourself past a breaking point. Susan David, host of the podcast *Checking In*, says this about self-compassion:

We all now run faster, work harder, stay up later, and multitask more aggressively, just to keep up—even in a pandemic. In this environment in which we're expected to approach life like an endless Ironman or Ironwoman competition, showing yourself self-compassion can be seen as a sign that you lack ambition or don't care about success as much as the next person does. There's a misconception that you need to be tough on yourself to maintain your edge. But people who are more accepting of their own failures may be more motivated to improve. Self-compassionate people aim just as high as self-critical people do. The difference is that self-compassionate people don't fall apart when, as sometimes happens, they don't meet their goals. (David 2020)

An essential element of self-compassion is treating yourself with care and understanding instead of judgment. Our internal critics are hardwired to point out all the things we have done wrong or where we fell short.

Showing compassion for oneself is a radical act.

One of the things that gets in the way of self-compassion is a belief we put on ourselves, whether consciously or unconsciously, that we need to be perfect. We should not fail. If we fail, we are failures.

The expectation of perfection only sets us up for failure again and again.

Until we start recognizing the need for self-compassion, we will put ourselves through this struggle repeatedly.

Take a moment to check in and grade yourself honestly. How well do you practice self-compassion?

Some ways to assess:

- Are you being harder on yourself than you are on others?
- Would you have more forgiveness and leniency for your failure if it happened to someone else?
- Would you say the same critical thing you're thinking to someone else? If not, then why are you saying it to yourself?

If you don't feel like you would give yourself a good grade, this is another moment for you to practice some compassion. This skill requires unlearning previous lessons you may have been taught.

Just like when you started playing a new sport or learned to play an instrument, the act of practicing self-compassion may initially feel awkward and disjointed. The more you do it, the more facility in it you will gain. This is not something you can read a book about and suddenly master. You need to get out and do it.

I also like to use what I call the "Rule of 10" when a challenge comes up and bothers me. I begin by asking myself these questions, in order, and see how far I get:

- Will this bother me in 10 minutes?
- Will this bother me in 10 hours?
- Will this bother me in 10 days?
- Will this bother me in 10 weeks?
- Will this bother me in 10 months?
- Will this bother me in 10 years?

For the record, I rarely make it beyond 10 days, and I don't think I recall anything that has taken me out to 10 months. This Rule of 10 is a way to help me recognize where I might be making something bigger in my mind than it really is. It helps me determine how much emotional energy and attention I want to put into it.

Even if I could create a quick fix that would give you exactly what you needed, I know that would not best serve you in the long run.

I have invested time practicing and building the muscles around self-compassion. They get stronger each time I do, and there is still room to make them stronger.

In order to develop greater emotional health, we need to:

- Expand our emotional range.
- Remember that emotions are not good or bad. How we respond to them may be.
- Remember that connection can promote good emotional health.
- Practice self-compassion.
- Use the "Rule of 10."

The final habit of the Whole Man is learning how to stay. This is the last step because you need to be doing all the previous things, and then as you are doing them, you must remember to remain. For me, this was one of the hardest habits to make a part of my regular practice. It was also the one that has created a lasting impact on me throughout my journey.

CHAPTER 9

STAY

As a parent, I am aware that my daughter is growing up, but a part of me still sees her as that little girl who I remember from years before. She is twelve (going on sixteen), and a situation came up that I needed to have a conversation with my ex-wife about. For anyone who has a preteen child, you know there are several potential topics, and this one was a biggie. As the conversation with my ex unfolded, I found myself getting triggered and scared.

Now I want you to understand there are several areas of my life where it has been easier for me to stay, yet one that I struggled with and continue to struggle with at times is in bringing more vulnerability with my ex-wife as we work to co-parent our daughter.

Looking back on it now, my little girl was growing up faster than I think I was ready for. I recognized I was getting emotional and made the choice to share that with my ex during our phone conversation. I started getting choked up. I resisted the urge to bottle it up and step over it.

As I shared what was going on for me, I started crying. My ex simply listened and let me finish. Afterward, she acknowledged how I was feeling and thanked me for being open and sharing what was going on with me in that moment. She said she appreciated seeing that side of me.

I know I was grateful that she hadn't tried to fix me or make me feel better when I shared what I did. I recognized that because I made the choice to stay and be in the middle of what was going on for me, it allowed us to have a stronger connection in our co-parenting journey.

Making the choice to stay will not always be easy.

What helps is the willingness to lean into the discomfort, remember the bigger picture, and focus on the relationships. Let's dive deeper into each of these.

The context I hold around staying is not hiding or running away from the difficulties in life. When something uncomfortable happens, we stay instead of submitting to that defensive reaction. Staying requires a commitment to growth and connection instead of a commitment to comfort and numbing.

Lean into Discomfort

When I think about demonstrating more vulnerability, I don't know that I would ever associate the words easy or comfortable with doing so. It requires us to step out of our comfort zone when we allow ourselves to be more open.

Part of growth is going beyond the borders of what feels comfortable or safe. What usually happens when we get outside our comfort zone and return is that we find it has grown.

With that growth comes the capacity to step even further beyond those boundaries next time, and one day we look up to realize how far we have come from where we started.

Discomfort will show up in different ways for everyone.

For some, it appears as a hesitancy to do that thing you know you need to do. It may be anxiety or worry that it won't go the way you want it to. One of my personal favorites is finding all those other things I need to do instead of doing what I really need to take care of right this moment. Yes, procrastination is a close cousin of avoiding. You already know which ones show up for you, and with that awareness, you can then make the choice to avoid the discomfort.

You can make the choice to start leaning in.

When we start practicing, it is good to do so with people who you have already established a level of trust and safety with. I do not suggest jumping in and doing this with complete strangers as you're finding your way.

Ease into it, kind of like dipping a toe into the pool water to test the temperature. Know that for some people, the comfort zone they need to step out of is around being with strangers, in which case dive right in!

I have also witnessed examples in the training courses I lead of men displaying vulnerability and openness. It is always well received, and some of those men are surprised when the women acknowledge how much they appreciate it. More than a few of those women have also commented about how they wish the men in their lives could be more open like that.

In early 2021, I was leading a coach training course, and in one exercise, I was acting as the client while participants practiced some of the coaching skills they were learning. The topic they were coaching me on brought up a lot of emotion, and at one point, I felt tears welling up inside me. I let them out without hesitation.

As we were debriefing the exercise, one of the men in the class acknowledged the impact seeing me express my emotions so openly had on him. He spoke of how he had never seen anything like that in a group setting, and certainly not from anyone who was in a leadership or teaching role. He told me he walked away from that experience feeling like he had more permission for himself to be with and to express his emotions because of what he had seen me do.

The experience reminded me once again that when I allow myself to bring greater vulnerability into learning spaces like that, the impact it creates is in giving others permission to be more open and vulnerable themselves.

When people comment on my willingness to show up vulnerably, they tend to start with things like, "That was brave," or, "You were courageous." I appreciate that. I know being vulnerable in those spaces can take courage.

A part of me also longs for the day when being vulnerable isn't something courageous for a man to do—where it is instead viewed simply as a part of how we see men and know they can show up. That it becomes the rule instead of the exception in how we expect and allow men to act.

Remember the Bigger Picture

When you are working to push through the discomfort, remembering why you are doing it is important. In his talk, "How Great Leaders Inspire Action," Simon Sinek introduces us to the importance of connecting with our "why" and how it can be a powerful connector.

Simon defines the "why" of his model as the leader truly understanding why they do what they do (Sinek 2009). Beyond what they do and how they do it, they know at their core why they are up to the task.

My "why" of wanting to be more open comes down to one word: *connection*. As humans, we are hardwired for connection. We form groups and societies to be in a community with one another. At our core, we are social creatures—so why fight it?

Parenting is a great reminder of the value of remembering the big picture. As my daughter has been growing up over the years, there have been many opportunities for me to come back and connect with what the bigger picture is that I want for her. Ultimately, I want to raise her to be a good citizen of the world and to have confidence in herself.

When I focus on that "why," it helps me avoid the trap of getting sucked into a reaction to whatever is going on in that moment and be able to think about how I need to respond or act in order to fulfill that higher goal I have.

My daughter has been taking piano lessons for several years (and yes, I'm a proud Papa for how amazing of a musician she has become!). In the last year or so, she started to get lax about regularly practicing each day. Initially, I fell into the trap of asking her each day or reminding her to practice. It became work for me, and I am certain she didn't appreciate my badgering about it.

I stopped for a moment to think about what I really wanted to accomplish in this, and realized I wanted to have her learn some self-discipline as I knew how important that would be later in life. When I connected with that, I shifted the conversation with her.

Instead of continually asking her about it, I sat down with her one day and told her, "I'm not going to keep asking you about practicing piano. You get to decide whether you do or not, and ultimately will live with the choices you make and the results you get."

And I stopped asking about her practicing. (I'm not going to say it was easy… I did have to bite my tongue more than a few times.)

Some days I knew she didn't practice, and I stuck to my guns. A week or two later, she got some feedback from her music teacher that one of her solos wasn't up to par, and she'd have to repeat it with some corrections. When I asked my daughter how she was doing, she said she felt bad because she knew she could do better. She admitted she hadn't been practicing regularly and knew that was why her solo was off.

She said she didn't want to fall behind the rest of the class and would start practicing regularly, and I told her I'd be happy to support her if she ever needed help.

Skipping piano practice hasn't been a problem since.

I could have continued harping on her practicing, but ultimately I was able to have a more significant impact by stepping back to see the bigger picture.

Another consideration is to not be attached to how others will respond when you open up. As I mentioned earlier, judgment often gets in the way of us being more open. This was true for me early on. In moments where I would work up the courage to show some vulnerability, I became hyper-aware of the responses of other men I interacted with. When someone would withdraw or seem bothered by my show of vulnerability, I would pull back.

I have come to realize that focusing on their response and acceptance of my openness was holding me back. Having spent as much time as I do practicing this, I now realize their response has nothing at all to do with me.

Their level of comfort or discomfort with it is part of their own journey.

By understanding and accepting this, it has allowed me to let go of any expectation of how others respond. Being unattached gives me the freedom to fully express myself independently from how others view or judge my actions. If I encounter moments where I forget this learning, I come back to my bigger picture or my why.

Look at places or relationships in your own life where you aren't getting the results you'd like.

Are you so focused on the specifics that you can't see the bigger picture? If that might be the case, take a moment to gain some distance and think about the long-term results you'd want.

Sometimes we get so focused on the issue that we forget about the importance of relationships.

Focus on Relationship

I believe relationships are incredibly easy and simple.

That is, until you involve another person. Then it becomes *way* more complicated.

The Whole Man recognizes that we are constantly in a relationship with ourselves and with others. Relationships with others can include family, friends, romantic partners, coworkers—the list goes on. When you go to the grocery store, and the teller is ringing up your purchase, in that moment, you are in a relationship with that person.

In each relationship we encounter in our lives, we learn new lessons about ourselves and those around us. Those lessons influence our actions and behaviors in future relationships, sometimes for the better and sometimes for the worse.

I find it interesting that in each new relationship you enter, these lessons are brand new and unique.

There may be similarities between this person and a person you knew before, yet they are not the same. It is important to remember to *interact with the person there in front of you in this moment* as opposed to the stories and experiences you have and hold of someone who might be similar that was in a relationship with you in the past.

For the men who struggle at times with showing greater vulnerability in a relationship, I offer this insight from Mark Manson:

"Connecting with others in this way by being vulnerable—as opposed to overcompensating and trying to get everyone to like you—will result in some of the best interactions and relationships of your life." (Manson)

I have discovered in all of my relationships, romantic or otherwise, when I allow myself to be more open, it creates deeper connections and interactions with those people. When I focus on the bigger picture of greater connection and lean into the discomfort that might arise, I am able to be more open with others and allow them to be more open with me.

Letting go of control is also required when you are focusing on a relationship. I don't know about you, but I have yet to encounter a "perfect" relationship.

As human beings, we are imperfect, and the crazy idea of expecting perfection from others only sets us up for disappointment and failure.

The Whole Man recognizes that he needs to interact with the person there in front of him in that moment, instead of the version from a day, a week, or a year ago.

Years ago, a friend of mine introduced me to the concept of "training your world in how to be with you." It is a way of taking responsibility for yourself and your world, and a way of setting expectations for how people interact with you. Up until this moment, your world has been responding to you based on how you have been showing up.

You are continually changing (as are the people in your world). They may not always be aware of the changes happening in you and may interact with the way they last encountered you.

Your responsibility is to help them see and understand the version of you here in this moment, thereby training them on how to be with you.

As you start practicing the habits of the Whole Man, you will begin to show up differently, and your world may not be ready for it or may not recognize those changes. This is where you take responsibility for helping them navigate this new direction you are going in.

Sometimes it will require you to remove or minimize relationships that aren't healthy for you or to discard the ones that are not helping you evolve into the man you want to become. At other times it will require you to ask for compassion from your world as you are practicing these new habits.

Speaking for what you need in support from your world can be a courageous act.

One of the greatest gifts of staying is that it keeps us from becoming isolated. When we can lean into discomfort, remember the bigger picture, and focus on the relationships we are creating and maintaining, it results in deeper and more meaningful connections in our world.

In the moments where we feel the weight of life and responsibilities, we know we have others we can lean on and lean into as support. When we stay, we get to experience the real magic of our common humanity.

Staying is a muscle we must continue strengthening. I have learned for myself that it was one of the toughest to develop.

It can be easy to want to shy away when it feels vulnerable and risky. I lived a good portion of my life afraid to stay. It wasn't a very fulfilling life. I know now that as I am able to stay more comfortably, it is deepening the relationships I have. Most importantly, I'm helping others feel a little safer in their own version of staying.

There you have it, the Habits of the Whole Man.

- Curiosity
- Awareness
- Presence
- Emotional Health, and
- Stay

Each of these habits impact, influence, and interact with one another. Remember that you need to begin by working through them individually, and know that some balance is also needed. When you can regularly practice all the habits, it creates more stability and wholeness.

Begin with the habits that speak to you, and then work to incorporate others as you go.

When combined, they help you step into a fuller, healthier perspective on masculinity.

They take time and effort. Remember that it is not about perfection—instead, it's about seeking mastery. Work to get better at each a little more every day, and you'll begin to understand the true benefit of being a Whole Man.

BUILDING AND SUSTAINING A WHOLE LIFE

CHAPTER 10

WORK INSIDE OUT

———

Just like Julie Andrews sings in *The Sound of Music*, we must start at the beginning, since it's a very good place to start.

To practice the habits of the Whole Man, you must start working from the inside out.

You begin by building the foundation solidly so that everything that gets erected above it has a firm base to rest upon.

It's an Inside Job

For several years of my professional career, I taught Stephen Covey's *The 7 Habits of Highly Effective People*. The content is immensely powerful, and the first three habits focus on self-mastery, which is moving oneself away from dependence to independence. I share this here because habit two, "begin with the end in mind," is integral to this work of becoming a Whole Man. You need to get a clear picture and vision of who you want to be if you ever hope to become that man.

What is your end in mind? Where do you want to go?

I spent several years as a project manager in the construction industry. Part of my job included overseeing tower cranes being installed on job sites to support new buildings being erected. I never fully understood the engineering and science that went behind how these cranes could be built so tall and lift the loads they did, yet I knew and appreciated that the most critical component was the foundation upon which they were built.

The calculations for those were double and triple checked by people with big, ten-pound brains. When the calculations were done right, it allowed those cranes to climb hundreds of feet in the air and safely move materials around job sites.

The same is true for building and sustaining the Whole Man life. Just as those tower cranes I worked with could lift incredibly heavy loads and move them all over the place, they needed to have a solid foundation to anchor them. If the foundation wasn't properly built, they could never fully achieve their true potential.

You need to make sure that you have a solid foundation to build upon, and if the foundation isn't solid, then you will make sure to spend the necessary time shoring it up.

Only you will be able to gauge if your foundation is solid as it currently exists, or if it still needs work. Take the time to assess this honestly; you will be doing yourself a great favor. Shortcut it, and you'll quickly find that things begin crumbling down.

The weight loss/diet control market and the fitness industry generate nearly $90 billion each year in the United States alone. Of that figure, weight loss and diet control make up more than two-thirds of it. What concerns me is that a lot of the messaging coming from that industry focuses on our outward appearance. We are continually sold the idea of the quick-fix, miracle solution that will make us look better or feel better in an instant.

I've learned that there are no shortcuts when it comes to self-work. Yes, taking care of your body is important, and as a Whole Man, you need to start from the inside and be willing to give it the time it requires.

In my conversation with Jim Young on an episode of *The Vulnerable Man* podcast, he shared a story from his life that contributed to his transformation:

> I often describe it as a full-scale rebuild. My life had been torn down to the studs. And it was time to do something about it. I had seen my dad collapse inward in the aftermath of his divorce; I was two when my parents divorced. So, I didn't see it unfold. But in retrospect, I saw that this man who—who helped raise me, really went away in that circumstance. And he's remained a distant figure in my life and pretty closed off to most people in the world.
>
> And so I knew I didn't want to go in that direction, what I realized was, okay, it's time to start doing something different. And the very first thing that I did was I went to therapy, and I got some mental health help and support. So that was the first layer of my rebuild. And then along the way, I encountered somebody who suggested to me, you know, "Hey, I know some of your story. And I know that you've dealt with a lot of people in your life that have addiction. And this program might be a place where you can find some support," and he invited me to attend an Al-Anon meeting with him.
>
> For those who aren't familiar with that, that Al Anon is a program for people who are in relationship

with addicts, usually alcoholics. And I knew that I was interested because I saw what this person had access to. In his life, he had this serenity, this peace, he was somebody who I felt was very wise. And so I said, "Well, I'll go check it out."

And I walked into this room about eight years ago. And I was in there for about twenty minutes. Hearing people start to share reading stories, and I said, I'm home. I'm in a place where people are just like me. And I could hear people sharing these incredibly vulnerable stories about what was going on in their life. And nobody was judging them. People were reaching out to support them in ways that didn't fix them, but just honored that they were showing up with a story that they were working through. And I thought, Oh, this is what I need, right?" (Veal 2010)

Taking care of our physical health is important and can contribute to a healthier sense of self-esteem. I'm not saying that we all need to become gym rats and strive to be on the cover of a fitness magazine, but being more active matters. In a 2016 study, researchers found that physical activity was directly associated with self-esteem. (Sani, Brand, et al. 2016)

Those who had spent some time working on themselves starting from an internal aspect tended to suffer less from burnout and external stresses. Whether they augmented it through therapy, group work, or personal development, they had all understood they needed to strengthen their internal foundation before they could make lasting changes in their external life. This is a hallmark of the Whole Man.

Pace Yourself

Growth and change are good things, and much like the rest of life, practicing moderation is important. You will have moments where you see big gains, and it feels like a lot of change is happening in a noticeably short time. Then there will be times when that progress slows to a crawl. I constantly remind myself that there will be ebbs and flows, and that things may sometimes feel stagnant. Regardless, there's value to all of it.

Remember that change starts within.

When I began my Whole Man journey, I was very eager. Once I started seeing the value I was gaining, I became hungry for more and more. The enthusiasm kept me motivated to move forward, and I needed to be reminded of the importance of moderation.

Trying to do too much, too fast, is a recipe for disaster. We are just like the tower cranes I mentioned earlier; we have limits we're evaluated to, and in order to perform properly, you have to know those limits.

We also need to remember that pacing plays a part. Real change takes place over time, and we need to remember patience.

One of the traps I have fallen into from time to time is comparing my progress to that of others. I look around and see some of the changes that others are going through, and my inner critic jumps up and starts to question why I am not moving at the same rate as they are. Nothing good can come from that.

When I was completing my coach training, I often compared myself to some of the people I saw leading the training courses. I would beat myself up mentally for not having greater mastery of coaching skills or not noticing things from my clients. That only gave my inner critic more fuel for breaking me down.

I'm fortunate to have people around me who help keep me grounded and remind me regularly that we're all moving at our own pace. My coach would often help me reground by reminding me that while I was only a few months into honing my skills, some of the people I was comparing myself to had been doing it for decades.

When you are in those moments where you are getting traction and making good headway, take advantage of it. Ride that momentum and enjoy it. Don't let yourself be sidetracked by thoughts of when it will end or when the momentum will subside.

Paying attention to what circumstances helped create the momentum for you is also important. Is it something you are doing? Is it people you are with? Is it something else? Whatever it may be, look for opportunities to recreate that situation in the future.

This is another place where leaning into your community can be helpful. Connecting with people who move at a similar pace or even one slightly ahead of where you are currently can help get you moving again as well. If you are already moving, it can help you increase your speed.

Sometimes you will need to consciously slow down. Do not ignore these moments.

Pace also includes knowing when to stop and take a breather—to relax and enjoy this moment and the scenery that's here.

If this sounds like a foreign concept to you, then I suggest you go back and read the chapter about presence one more time.

Tuning in to rhythm will help you with pacing. Our bodies will have a natural rhythm that may dictate the levels of energy we have for the things we're doing. You have highs and lows throughout each day, and you may also notice similar variations across a week or even a month.

Being aware of those rhythms can help you leverage when that energy is higher, which can help increase the gains you're getting. Similarly, knowing when that energy is lower, it may be important for you to not push yourself and allow time for introspection.

Music is a structure I sometimes use to help enhance or influence my pace. When you walk into my house, you can tell pretty quickly what kind of mood I'm in based on the music playing. Sometimes it is more relaxed and chilled; other times, it's up-tempo and more energetic.

When I go to the gym to work out, I use certain playlists to help keep me motivated and focused. Those playlists are drastically different from when I'm sitting on the couch reading a book.

I have learned to tune in to what I need in the moment and then find what I need to support that.

In his article, "Why You Need to Pace Yourself," Matt Crossman says, "If we try to go full speed all the time… we'll never make it to the finish line. We need to pace ourselves mentally, physically, and emotionally, or we'll burn out" (Crossman 2020). The article is a great example of the value found in collaborating and working with others. It reasons that whether operating solo or with others, we need to be aware of ourselves and the pace we're driving ourselves at.

Scratch, Begin Again

As you continue the journey, you may fail at times.

You probably don't want to hear that, but it's just reality.

When you can, take a do-over—a mulligan. I like to use the term "scratch, begin again" when that happens. When you try something, and it doesn't work the way you hoped it would—don't beat yourself up about it. Instead, look for the learning opportunity it created for you.

Then take that learning and apply it for the next attempt.

It's another way of looking through the lens of, "Well, there's one way that didn't work out," and then leaning into the earlier habits of curiosity and awareness. We continually go through this cycle, and each moment is an experience in our life that gives us a chance to continue to learn more.

"Scratch, begin again" reminds me of John C. Maxwell's book, *Failing Forward*. In the book, one of the key messages I took away was about reframing how we look at failing or failure. Many people default to the perspective that failure is a negative thing—that it's a reflection of who we are. That is because the messaging we tend to hear when we are growing up reinforces the mindset that we must succeed continually.

We have structures placed around us at an early age that continually remind us about competition with others. In school, we receive grades, and the goal is to have higher grades because that means you are succeeding. Sports have a winner and a loser, and while people talk about the importance of sportsmanship, what gets celebrated in the media is those who win.

Shifting our thinking around the idea of failing can change failure into a powerful learning tool for noting a way that something doesn't work. It can be a catapult to a new and better way for us if we choose to look for the lesson in the experience.

Of all the people I've spoken to who have become successful in any area of their lives, not one of them says they achieved what they did on the first try. They all stumbled and failed. They fell down, they tried, and they missed the mark. Then they got up and tried it again—and again, sometimes dozens or hundreds of times, until they succeeded.

The idea of perfection gets in the way of us embracing failure. For many years, my perfectionist got in the way of me even attempting big goals because I told myself that if I didn't get it "just right," I had failed.

When I began my journey as a coach, the overachiever in me constantly beat me up for any missteps or stumbles I had along the way. My coach gave me a great approach which transformed how I showed up as a coach.

She said, "Seek *mastery*, not *perfection*." Those four words carried so much weight. It allowed me to let go of there being a right or wrong about it, and instead work to improve and get better every day. As I continue to work at mastering my craft, I can do so without that internally driven pressure to get it perfect.

An element of playfulness or lightness exists in "scratch, begin again." If you watch kids play, they are a perfect example of this. I remember when my daughter was younger, I had bought her some LEGO. I remembered as a kid how much I enjoyed playing with them and wanted to share that experience with her as well. The first time we got them out, we both spread out on the floor in her room and began stacking the various shaped bricks.

At one point, I looked over, and she had started constructing something that went in all kinds of different directions. It fell over more than once, and sometimes parts broke off. For a split second, I thought about offering her a tip to help it look more consistent or be more stable, and instead, I caught myself. I recognized that she wasn't attached to what it needed to look like and was creating as she went.

Several times, she tried putting things together, and they didn't work. And instead of getting frustrated or upset that she hadn't done it right, she simply tried something different.

This continues to be a reminder for me to view things in a "childlike way." To help me see things from a fresh and open-minded perspective. I invite you to try it as well and see what it opens you up to.

I want to remind you of the element of compassion again. As you are growing and learning, you need to have compassion for yourself as you stumble and fall.

When a young child is first learning to walk and they fall, we would never tell them to just give up and stop trying. We wouldn't say, "Bad baby, you're not good at walking. You should just give up trying."

Of course not. We encourage them; we celebrate each extra step they take that they didn't before. Yet, for some reason, when *we* try new things, we are much harder on ourselves than we ever would be on others, or than they would be on us.

We need to adjust that mindset as we work to change how we are holding and demonstrating healthy masculinity.

Working from the inside out requires you to start from the inside, building up from the foundation. You need to pace yourself and know when to push forward and when to ease up. Finally, you need to be willing to stumble and fail, while learning along the way so that you can find the path that works for you. Heck, it might be an elevator or a slide instead of a path.

In the next chapter, we will talk about finding allies to support you in your journey as you connect to community.

CHAPTER 11

FIND YOUR TRIBE

Have you ever found yourself sitting amongst a group of people, scratching your head, and wondering how you ended up there with such strange people with whom you have difficulty relating?

Or maybe it's the opposite; you think back to some people whose company just felt "right," like being at home.

If either of these resonated with you, then you understand the concept of community.

I sometimes use the word tribe to represent community, and the definition that stands out for me is: "A group of persons having a common character, occupation, or interest." In particular, I'm focused on the common character or interest.

You may belong to several different communities. I have one community of men who are fathers. I have another of my fellow Marines and a broader community of veterans and service members. I have one of the coaches and leadership development professionals I've met. I've also discovered that I have a community of men (and women) who want to evolve the way we hold masculinity. (By the way, thanks for joining… you didn't know that membership was included with the book—bonus!)

Each one represents a facet of who I am or have been at some point in my life, and they support me in different ways.

Connect to Community (or Build It!)

When the world fell into the grips of the pandemic in early 2020, many of us went into survival mode and began focusing on what was closest to home, minimizing how much we were connecting with others in the process. While that was happening, some found a greater desire for building more connections, instead of closing them off.

One such man was Jamie Robins. When I interviewed him on October 21, 2021, for this book, he shared how he and Phil Askew came to build their "Safe Harbour" community for men.

> And me and Phil were doing the daily check in. We were doing this check in where we use our WhatsApp; we press record. And we do three minutes each day. I check in with him three minutes; he checks me three minutes. And you know how that works. No judgment—no. Doesn't matter if you call me back, kind of stuff. And those check ins started getting longer. Five minutes, six minutes. I think the record was about nineteen minutes during that time. And I'm in my own men's group at this point, which I had been in for about three years. Regular men's group, same guys, seven guys.
>
> And then after that one circle up I messaged Phil and say, "We've got to do something. We've got to create a men's circle for any man who wants to come and do

this, and we have to do it online because of COVID." And he just went, "Right let's do it." And twenty minutes later he'd emailed me back a logo… He'd, fuckin' done it, you know. Boom, this thing comes up. Got this great idea. We'll call it Safe Harbor. Brilliant name. And we'll set it up for next Friday. And I'll put it out in the CTI Facebook group. And within twenty-four hours we filled out seven or eight seats something like that. And that's how it started. And then we did one.

And then I thought I have to keep this going. I have to because it's not—it's okay to just do one a one off, but this has to be a regular thing. So, I decided that it would be every week.

So we did it every Thursday night. And men showed up. It was a bit slow at first, but men showed up. And regular men would show up every time. (Veal 2021)

What I loved about this is that Jamie recognized the power of community and the impact it had on him, and when he couldn't find it in the way he needed it, he chose to do something about it.

Community has been one of the greatest supports and motivators for me in this journey to becoming a Whole Man. When I started out, I thought I was the only man (or, at least, one of the only men) doing this kind of work. Thankfully, the community I have found continues to show me that isn't true—not by a long shot.

During the first few years of interviewing men around the topic of vulnerability, I had convinced myself that finding men to talk on the subject was going to be difficult. I found that men who I talked to or interacted with in other parts of my world started referring people for me to speak with.

One clear reminder that the universe sent my way was when a colleague of mine made virtual introductions to seven different men in one day. He and I had spoken about what I was doing with this work, and he immediately rattled off these people he wanted to connect me with. I told him I appreciated the introductions. A little part of me was skeptical because these seven men had no idea who I was; the only common link we had was this friend.

Within four hours of those first email introductions being sent, all seven responded with an enthusiastic yes to join me in being interviewed.

This became just one more reminder about how much men crave to be in this conversation. The more we create opportunities where it is safe for them to talk about these things, the more they will show up and participate.

I have mentioned that humans are social creatures, and we are naturally drawn toward being together. This helped some of our earliest ancestors survive, and even today, we are naturally drawn to connecting with people with whom we share interests.

Oddly enough, when it comes to talking about vulnerability for men, we often tell ourselves we must do it alone. We convince ourselves that this is a journey we must walk individually and that leaning on others is some kind of unspoken injustice.

That belief system of having to do it alone undermines the power of community. Because we are taught and continue to hold on to this idea that as men, we can't ask for help, it keeps us isolated. It doesn't allow us to gain the full benefit that can be derived from being connected to others.

In David Logan's "Tribal Leadership" TEDx Talk, he talks about the different tribes we form and are drawn to, alongside the five levels in each tribe. He explains how as leaders in our respective tribes, we have a responsibility to recognize what level we are at and also help to move our tribe forward a level (Logan 2009).

Stage One: "Life Sucks"
Stage Two: "My Life Sucks"
Stage Three: "I'm great (and you're not)"
Stage Four: "We're Great"
Stage Five: "Life is Great"

The most effective leaders can speak to people at each of the five levels in a way their message will be heard. Evaluating which of the levels your tribe (or tribes) are at and asking yourself how your tribe will make a meaningful impact is important.

Something else to keep in mind is the idea that you may find community in places you hadn't expected. Some groups will be obvious to you. Keeping an open mind can help you find new groups you might have otherwise overlooked.

My journey in creating my podcast has been a very real example for me. I have been able to connect with communities that I wouldn't have found had it not been for the podcast.

On my journey of writing this book, I found out how nurturing and supportive a community of writers can be. I always thought of writing as a solitary experience. What I came to realize is that having writers I could speak with on a regular basis enhanced my writing process and normalized my writing experience. It lessened the pain of moments of writers' block. Celebrating reaching milestones such as getting green-lit for publication was also great!

The fact they were writing on subjects vastly different from my book didn't matter one bit. Empathizing, sympathizing, and sometimes just flat out complaining about the struggle held power. Knowing there was support helped keep me focused. One fellow author I connected with was writing a book about executive recruiting. I know nothing about that topic… and that doesn't matter. We spent time talking about our respective book-writing journeys, which created a beautiful connection in the moment.

I encourage you to set aside time and think about the tribes you're in. Think about the value you get and give from being in them. Are they helping to build you up, or do they hold you back from achieving your potential?

If it's the former, celebrate and support them. If it's the latter, it might be time to find a new tribe.

And if that new tribe doesn't exist, start it.

Be like Jamie and Phil and create the community you'd want to be a part of.

Speak Up and Speak Out

Speaking up and speaking out is about sharing your message and what you are up to with the people in your world.

I knew early on how important this work involving masculinity and vulnerability was to me. I suspected it was for other men as well. Yet, I was afraid to talk about it in certain circles. I was very curious and open about the subject and willing to lean into it myself, yet I continued to believe other men might not be as willing. This made me avoid directly using the word vulnerability when trying to engage men in the conversation.

Wrap your head around that for a moment. I wanted to talk to men about vulnerability yet didn't feel safe using the word—insanity! (As you can tell, I've since recognized that I had to be vulnerable in order to get started.)

When I would interact with groups of men and women, I might talk about being open, letting down your guard, or connecting within, instead of being straightforward and saying "vulnerability." These felt like ways to dance around the very thing I knew I wanted to talk about, yet I felt afraid that it would scare them away if I spoke about it directly.

As I witness my daughter beginning to explore new interests, I am reminded that from time to time, we make things scarier in our minds than they ever would be in real life. A few months ago, my daughter asked to volunteer and play some music at the place where she had done her piano group lessons. She was excited to go play for the classes yet also nervous about it.

She confided afterward that she had been really concerned about messing up and not playing well. Once she started playing, she was able to relax and enjoy it. It hadn't ended up being anywhere nearly as scary as her worry had created.

Life gave me another example to learn that very same lesson.

A couple of years ago, I started using the word vulnerable or vulnerability more often in my conversations with men. At first, I did it with hesitation, still worried they might withdraw or shrink away from me.

In the moments where I mustered up the courage to dive in, I most commonly would get knowing nods or smiles from those men, and many of them would lean forward and engage more deeply in the conversation.

It seemed counterintuitive until I realized that many men were seeking the space and permission to bring more vulnerability.

I facilitated training sessions and began mentioning how I was doing work to help men better connect with vulnerability. It would frequently be met with affirming comments from people—both men and women—sharing how they agreed that we needed more of this in the world.

Hearing these things emboldened me to continue doing it more.

The more I shared about this work I was doing, the more I found people wanting to support it and join in the conversation.

One surprise benefit of my speaking out is that people started connecting me with this subject of vulnerability. I had colleagues and previous clients referring people to me and calling me the "vulnerability guy."

They would share examples of how a conversation or coaching engagement with me helped them tap into more vulnerability and, as a result, have a more fulfilling life.

One of the biggest compliments I received was a little over a year ago when someone looked at me and said, "You're like the male version of Brené Brown!" I took that as a huge compliment. My inner critic also took that as a fantastic opportunity to beat me up a little bit for even daring to think of that as a possibility. The good news is that I'm not tuning in to that critical voice anymore (at least when it comes to that topic).

Something I learned as I began speaking up and speaking out more was that finding my own language around it was important. When I tried using the ways others might speak on the subject, it didn't always ring authentically for me, which made me hesitate to share my message.

The more I talked about it, the more I began to find my own words and way of sharing in a way that felt real for me. That helped me be more comfortable in starting the conversation with people I didn't know well or with whom I didn't have an existing relationship.

Another benefit of speaking was that it helped the people in my network and people I encountered know more about how I was trying to evolve the way we viewed masculinity. They became an extended network for me and were able to not just share my message; they also became a resource for connecting me with people whom I might not have otherwise encountered. Hello, growing my community!

While it wasn't on my radar when I started, as I began speaking up more, I realized I wanted to share this message with a greater audience. Not because I wanted *my* voice to be heard; rather, I wanted to celebrate the men I was meeting who were doing similar work and on their own journeys.

I know for myself that talking to scores of men along the way who had been doing their own work helped me gain insights on how I could do my own work. In the spring of 2020, I decided that one way I could help expand the reach of that message was to create a podcast.

Cue *The Vulnerable Man* podcast.

When I first thought about creating the podcast, a bunch of doubts jumped up. People asked me questions like:

- "How are you going to monetize it?"
- "How are you integrating it into your business and marketing?"
- "What is your listenership goal?"

These were all exceptionally good questions and, in all reality, ones that I should have spent a lot of time thinking about. The truth is I simply wanted to share conversations with like-minded people.

At certain times in my life, I can be more of a "ready, fire, aim" type of person, and this was certainly one of those situations. Don't get me wrong—there is a definite value in putting thought and planning into things that you are doing. I also knew that the podcast wasn't about generating revenue; it was about generating change.

I don't know about you, but I'm not entirely sure that you can always strategize and plan change. Sometimes it just happens once you act.

What I continue to be reminded of is that the more I speak up and share about the work and the impact I want to create, the more I find people to help share that message. It helps people recognize and recommend people with whom I should be in community.

Set the Structure

In coaching, we use the concept of a structure to help a client anchor in or integrate new learning they have had or awareness they have gained. It helps them connect to a commitment to action they have made or a behavior they want to practice. Some examples I've seen used might be:

- Changing the ringtone on their phone to a song that reminds them of when they are feeling powerful or confident.
- Setting a random timer or alarm to go off to help them take a moment, slow down, and take several deep breaths.
- Creating an "if/then" reward (e.g., if I finish the report for work, then I get to spend ten minutes browsing social

media). This can be particularly powerful when trying to break bad habits or create new ones.

- Placing post-it notes in your workspace to reinforce specific messages you want to remember.

The limits of what a structure can be are only bounded by your own imagination and creativity. The structure is meant to support you in connecting with something important.

You can use the idea of a structure to support you in staying connected to your learning as you journey toward becoming a Whole Man. I have found two that have been significantly helpful in keeping me grounded and connected.

One is my coach, Laura, and the other is the community of people I am consciously choosing to surround myself with and spend time with. Each helps me anchor myself in a unique way.

Structures do not need to be permanent; they can change and shift to suit your needs. You may find it useful to change them up from time to time, as variety keeps a freshness to them.

Begin by determining what you want to create the connection to or reminder for. Once you have that in mind, you can consider what would help you remember that idea in moments where you might normally forget.

Maybe a particularly challenging person triggers you when you have difficult conversations with them. In that case, you may create a structure that helps you settle yourself *before* you step into that conversation.

Another simple and enormously powerful structure that I like to share comes from Amy Cuddy's TED Talk "Your Body Language May Shape Who You Are." In it, she talks about the concept of "high power" and "low power" poses and shares the research she did on how the different poses can dramatically affect the testosterone and cortisol levels in the brain (Cuddy 2012).

High-power poses are expansive (taking up more space) and open (the limbs are held far away from the body), while low-power poses are constricted (taking up less space) and clenched (the limbs are held close/tight to the body).

Amy found that when people *adopted high power poses for just two minutes*, they had an increase in testosterone and a decrease in cortisol (a stress hormone), which resulted in increased confidence and willingness to take risks. The inverse was true for those who adopted low power poses.

I can speak firsthand about the impact it can create. About a year after I saw this talk, I was going in for a job interview. A few minutes before my scheduled time, instead of sitting in the lobby in a chair (and likely in a low-power pose), I went into the restroom and locked myself in a stall for two minutes while I adopted a high-power pose.

An hour later, as I left the interview, I felt confident I had given a clear representation of who I was and what I could bring to the position, and a part of me knew I had nailed it.

A week later, I was extended an offer for the position.

I can't guarantee that doing the high-power poses will get you that job or help you land that deal you're chasing. What I do know is that in my own experience, it has definitely helped decrease my feelings of stress when I do them. Give it a try; what have you got to lose?

It does not matter what structure you decide to create. What matters is finding something that will support you. I am a big advocate of a coach being a powerful structure to support you, and not just because it's part of the work I do. For the last several years, I have had a coach, and I will continue to have one because I have seen firsthand the value it generates for me.

Finding your tribe is a part of how you will build and sustain a Whole Man life.

You do that by connecting to community and like-minded people, speaking up and speaking out about what matters to you, and then finding a structure to help you continue building toward the person you want to become.

I like to say that "*we* can accomplish far more than I ever can alone." When I am connected with others, I get to witness the truth of that. In the final chapter, we will dive into how you can use everything covered to this point to help you live a whole life.

CHAPTER 12

LIVING WHOLE

I struggled for a long time with giving myself permission to let my authentic light shine, and it cost me. I altered who I was to show up how I thought others expected me to. I felt frustration resulting from relationships that weren't serving me and from work that didn't fulfill me and feed my soul.

And most of all, I played small in my life, not allowing myself to dream as big as I wanted to.

Build the Habits

I previously introduced you to the habits of the Whole Man:

- Curiosity—being in the question and open to exploring.
- Awareness—knowing where you are and where you want to go on your journey.
- Presence—slowing down and connecting with this moment and being present with others.
- Emotional Health—practicing emotional wellness.

- Stay—remaining, especially when it becomes uncomfortable.

As you practice the habits, you will have days where you will succeed and move forward. You will also have times when you don't. Researchers have studied habit and habit formation for years, and one of the commonly held beliefs is that when we are trying to adopt a new habit, we need to practice it for about twenty days before it really starts to stick.

In his book *Atomic Habits*, James Clear shares the idea of consistent, 1 percent incremental improvements that lead to big changes over time. He says:

> Habits are the compound interest of self-improvement. The same way that money multiplies through compound interest, the effects of your habits multiply as you repeat them. They seem to make little difference on any given day, and yet the impact they deliver over the months and years can be enormous. It is only when looking back two, five, or perhaps ten years later that the value of good habits and the cost of bad ones become strikingly apparent. (Clear 2018)

Before I go any further, I want to highly recommend that if you haven't read this book, go pick it up (but finish reading this one first!). James offers a lot of great and easy-to-implement tools and techniques to help you make lasting change that yields big results.

His idea of habit stacking was crucial to helping me write this book.

With habit stacking, you take a habit you are already doing on a regular basis, and you attach the new habit you are trying to create to it. In my case, every morning, I get up and make coffee. My habit of sitting down with that cup of coffee as I started my day was the one that I leveraged to create the new habit and make it stick.

My new habit kicked in as soon as I sat down at my computer with that cup of coffee. Instead of jumping into emails or surfing the web, I would spend at least thirty minutes writing and capturing ideas for my book. For the first few weeks, I had to consciously think about starting the second habit as I sat down with my cup of coffee, and eventually, it happened automatically.

As you continue building your habits, it helps to keep in mind the four stages of adult learning, sometimes called the four stages of competence. Noel Burch outlines this as (Hirschi):

Four Stages of Adult Learning

- Unconscious Incompetence—you don't know what you don't know.
- Conscious Incompetence—you know what you don't know (or what you don't do well).
- Conscious Competence—you know what you know (you can perform the skill, but it takes attention and concentration).
- Unconscious Competence—you know it so well you don't think about doing it (you can perform the skill without thinking about it). We have created and strengthened the neural pathways enough that we don't have to put our attention to it.

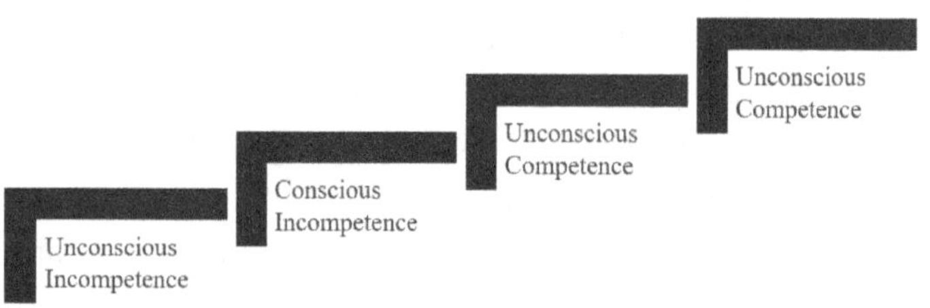

The example I use to illustrate this is driving a car. When you were a young child, say two or three years old, you didn't know that you didn't know how to drive a car as you sat in the back seat watching someone drive. That is *unconscious incompetence*. As you got older, you became aware that you didn't know how to drive a car. You could see your parent operating the controls to make the car do the things it did, yet you weren't fully aware of what it all meant. You had moved up to *conscious incompetence.*

When you took driver's education or driving lessons and began driving on your own, you entered *conscious competence.* You could get the car from point A to point B, but you had to consciously think about many of the steps involved.

As you practiced more and gained more experience, you may have moved to the point of *unconscious competence.* Perhaps you left your house one day driving somewhere, and sometime later arrived at your destination. You didn't have to put conscious thought into changing lanes, putting on your turn signal (yes, you are still supposed to do that), applying the brakes, or stepping on the gas. You were able to demonstrate these skills without having to specifically focus on them.

Another way to recognize that you may have reached conscious competence is the ability to teach it to others.

When we are learning new skills or trying new habits, we will spend a lot of time moving back and forth between conscious incompetence and conscious competence. There will be a lot of discomfort in this place, and it is also the space where the greatest learning and growth come for us.

In the previous chapter, we talked about pacing yourself, and that applies here as well. Remember that you do not have to master all these habits at once. Take your time and work through them. Allow them to build upon each other. Make use of the things that will help you move toward conscious competence in practicing these habits.

Celebrate the Wins and Losses

As I've mentioned, I have never run a marathon. I cannot conceive of any reality where I decide to in my lifetime, but one thing I can appreciate about marathon runners is that they are very good at gauging their progress in the midst of performing.

Growing up, a close friend of my mother's ran marathons several times a year. I remember her talking once about how she would time each mile she ran and could adjust on the fly to push herself where she needed so that she could finish in the time she was chasing after. She talked about some of the challenges and successes in her training before each marathon, and how there were days when she just physically couldn't train, and she found ways to work around that. She was capable of looking at her training from a big-picture perspective and able to zoom in and look at each individual session separately.

To live as a Whole Man, you need to adopt a similar mindset and be able to celebrate along the way.

I recently had a coaching call with a CEO with whom I had been working for several months. When we started working together, he was struggling with improving communication between his senior leaders. They did not trust each other deeply. As we were checking in at the beginning of the call, he shared his frustration that he felt like he was going around and around and that he hadn't made any notable progress over the last few months.

We took some time and had him look at how his team was currently functioning and then looked back to when we started working together. In that conversation, he realized that because he was so focused on where he thought he still needed to get to with growing the team, he hadn't made any real progress.

As he spoke about how the team was more proactive in their communication with each other, particularly about the way they had become closer, he recognized he had made a lot more progress than he was giving himself credit for.

He also realized one of the biggest factors in that shift was the way he started showing up as a leader. He was more open in his communication with his team and showed more vulnerability as a leader while he was doing it.

By him setting that example and modeling the behavior he was hoping to get from them, they were beginning to open up and connect with each other in ways they hadn't before.

I share this because we often lose sight of how far we've come toward reaching our goals or making the changes we desire.

Back in 2013, I set a goal to be selected to give a TED Talk. It seemed audacious and scary when I first spoke it out loud, and it was one of those moments where I wished I could have pulled those words back in. My coach wasn't going to let me off the hook that easy, and so it began. I applied and looked into TEDx events across the country, and in October the following year, I was selected to give my talk.

About a month before the event was due to happen, I was notified that I was being removed from the programming because my topic was a social issue and the event organizers wanted to focus on business issues.

Yes, I had a pity party for myself for a few days; I can't lie. I was angry, upset, and sad that I wasn't going to be able to fulfill the goal I'd set for myself.

After a few days of moping around, I got out of my funk and began looking for the learning in the experience.

I realized that I had accomplished my original goal: I set out to be *selected* to give a TED Talk. I was also able to reframe it from the perspective that the universe was testing my resolve around giving that talk.

You can bet that the new goal I set was to *deliver* my talk.

In May 2017, I marked that new one as complete when I stepped onto the red circle in Bend, Oregon, and delivered my talk.

Stopping from time to time and seeing where you are in your progress—while celebrating the wins and losses you have along the way—will help you on your journey to becoming whole.

Continue Evolving

Evolving who you are as a man and as a person is an ongoing journey. You will never get to a destination where you can kick your feet up, lean back, and say to yourself, "I'm here. Done. Nothing more to learn."

We will continually discover new areas about ourselves, the way we interact with and are in relationships with others, and how we show up in the world.

Our environments are continually changing around us. Today, we're living in a world that requires skills and abilities our ancestors couldn't even have dreamed of or imagined. We need to continue evolving and adapting to our environment if we want to thrive. Part of the adaptation that is desperately needed right now is a move toward healthier masculinity.

As men—and as a society—we need to regularly look at who we are and how we are behaving and evaluate that against where we need to go. If what we're doing today won't get us to where we want to be in the future, then we must adjust.

We will have times when that change happens rapidly. We will encounter plateaus where the status quo remains for a while. What matters is that we continually keep an eye on what that next element of evolution will look like.

The habits of the Whole Man are cyclical and repeating.

They are constantly in play and interacting and feeding each other. Individually, they help us shift. Collectively, they generate a synergistic effect that becomes exponential.

We cannot be complacent with how things have been done to this point. There is value in some of it, and there is room for us to grow and evolve. You have an active part in where we go from here.

You can't unlearn living as a Whole Man once you've discovered it. You are changed at the cellular level, even if the rest of your mind hasn't caught up with it.

When you connect with and regularly practice the habits of the Whole Man, you will have access to parts of yourself that have been yearning to come out.

You will have a deeper connection with the people in your life.

You will have a greater focus on the man you want to be and the impact you want to create.

Living whole carries freedom. Freedom from having to live a confined version of yourself.

Freedom from being tied to unhealthy masculinity.

It lets you step into the full power of who you are and who you are meant to be.

One of my favorite quotes is from Marianne Williamson, and I want to leave you with it as you embark on your Whole Man journey. I invite you to shine so that you inspire and give others permission to do the same. Help us collectively evolve masculinity so we can all be liberated.

> Our deepest fear is not that we are inadequate. Our deepest fear is that we are powerful beyond measure. It is our light, not our darkness, that most frightens us. We ask ourselves, "Who am I to be brilliant, gorgeous, talented, fabulous?" Actually, who are you not to be? You are a child of God. Your playing small does not serve the world. There is nothing enlightened about shrinking so that other people won't feel insecure around you. We are all meant to shine, as children do. We were born to make manifest the glory of God that is within us. It's not just in some of us; it's in everyone. And as we let our own light shine, we unconsciously give other people permission to do the same. As we are liberated from our own fear, our presence automatically liberates others.

I look forward to greeting you on the path.

ACKNOWLEDGMENTS

To all my family and friends who made this book possible, thank you. I especially want to thank my mother, who modeled vulnerability to me before I even understood what it was. I miss our conversations, mom.

To my best friend Dave, who contributed his artistic talents to the book cover, thank you for always having my back and being a constant reminder to keep a youthful spirit.

To my amazing coach, Laura Coyle, thank you for being on this journey all these years. Before I knew this book was in me, you were in my corner. Thank you, Laura.

Ilene, thank you for the encouragement, support, and cheerleading along the way. You're good to me and good for me.

Wash, you've been like a father figure to me all these years in a way I hadn't fully recognized. Thank you for showing me what it means for a man to have strength and vulnerability.

To all the men I've been fortunate enough to cross paths with on this journey, a huge thank you to you. Those who I've interviewed, had conversations with, or who simply impacted my own journey to becoming a Whole Man, words can't capture the depth of my gratitude.

I also want to thank the very generous group of individuals who purchased a copy of this book during the presale. You are the ones who made the publication of this story possible and reminded me of the power of leaning into community. Thank you for making an investment in the work I want to bring into the world. This group includes:

Aaron Foellmi, Aaronde Seckou Creighton, Alan Heymann, Alanna Gillis, Alexsis Veal, Alison Bishop, Alonso Raul Rios Garcia, Angela Vanhorn, Ann Farrell, Ave Peetri, Ben Hoffman, Bobby Barzi, Brian Dozer, Brian Young, Candice Yorke, Carlo Bos, Chad Knudson, Cheri Sherman, Chris Johns, Chris Murman, Christina McFadden, Christopher Glantz, Cynthia Loy Darst, Dave Vaught, David Atkins, David Evans, David Jungck, Donna Ghalambor, Ed Frauenheim, Emm Dungate, Eric Koester, Eric Kohner, Eric Scott, Everett Shupe II, Francis Quimby, Gene Washington, Henry Kimsey-House, Ilene Morse, James Young, Janice Lichtenwaldt, Jean Alexander, Jeff Jacobsen, Jill Medina Elizalde, Joanna Lane, Josh Phillips, Joshua Bruggink, Kaitlyn Corse, Karen Bordson, Kat Knecht, Kathy Laurnen, Kay Cooper, Ken Mossman, Kenny Dobbs, Kim Moriyama, Kimberly Sauceda (aka Slacker Senior,) Kvon Tucker, LaMont Bonham, Laura Coyle, Laura Lueder, Laurie Broadfoot (aka Cuz'n Lou,) Liberty Des Roches-Dueck, Lisa Hunefeld, Lynette Burgan, Madeleine Colliere, Maite Gonzalez Poveda, Margaret Walker Scavo,

Marjoleine Byrne, Mark Christensen, Mark Staelgraeve, Mark Van Ells, Marlena deCarion, Mary McGuinness, Matthew Goldman, Matthew Kirschner, Michael Carman, Michael Huckaby, Mike Hogg, Nanor Ohanesian, Natalie Vartanian, Nathan Knecht, Nicki Leaper, Nicole Garrett, Nita Ritzke, Pam Kowalski, Pat Carrington House, Quentin Finney, Rob "Tanner" Wortham, Robert Henrikson, Sara Baziotis, Scott Husband, Sean Harvey, Shee Van Inwegen, Stephanie Chin, Susan Fisher, Susan Retik, Tamaryn Boston, Tania Zeigler, Terry Sweeny, Tina-Marie Meyer, Travis Maruska, Travis Stock, William Broniec, and many others who choose to remain anonymous.

A special shout out to Jonathan Wilkinson for being an Author Champion, and to Angela Migliaccio for not only being an Author Champion, but also a huge supporter of *The Vulnerable Man* podcast and this work.

And Julie, just because. (You were the original Silly Rabbit.)

APPENDIX

————

Chapter 1

[none]

Chapter 2

Canadian Mental Health Association. "What if Negative Emotions Aren't So Bad?" May 3, 2021. https://cmha.ca/what-if-negative-emotions-arent-so-bad/

Eckman, Paul. "Universal Facial Expressions of Emotion." *California Mental Health Research Digest*Vol. 8 (Autumn 1970) No. 4; 151-158.

Eckman, Paul and Wallace Friesen. "Constants Across Cultures in the Face and Emotion." *Journal of Personality and Social Psychology* Vol 17, No. 2: 124-129.

Fritz, Ron. "An Exploration of Coming of Age Rituals & Rites of Passage in a Modern Era." Filmed May 2017 at TEDxBend, Bend, OR. Video, 18:31. http://tedxbend.com/presenters/ron-fritz/

The Representation Project. "SNEAK PEAK: Masculinity in Popular Culture." July 8, 2015. 5:40. https://youtu.be/6fh_ZPc29ks

Rodriguez, Tori. "Negative Emotions Are Key to Well-Being." *Scientific American* May 1, 2013. https://www.scientificamerican.com/article/negative-emotions-key-well-being/

Siebel Newsom, Jennifer, dir. *The Mask You Live In.* 2015; The Representation Project. DVD.

Chapter 3

Boot Camp for New Dads. https://www.bootcampfornewdads.org/

Veal, Christopher. "The Vulnerable Man Episode 38—Josh Levs." January 17, 2022. 54:42. https://vulnerableman.libsyn.com/vulnerable-man-ep038-josh-levs

Themaneffect.com. "What is Masculinity? That's a Question Every Man Should be Asking Himself." Aug. 18, 2019. http://themaneffect.com/thejourney/what-is-masculinity-thats-a-question-every-man-should-be-asking-himself

Chapter 4

The Good Men Project. "The Subtle Shaming of Men and Vulnerability." December 26, 2016. https://goodmenproject.com/sex-relationships/the-subtle-shaming-of-men-and-vulnerability-dg/

Wong, DW, KR Hall, CA Justice, and L Wong. *Counseling Individuals Through the Lifespan.* Sage Publications. 2014.

Chapter 5

Brown, Brené. "Listening to Shame." TED2012. March 2012. 20:22. https://www.ted.com/talks/brene_brown_listening_to_shame#t-1070666

Brown, Brené. "The Power of Vulnerability." TEDxHouston. June 2010. 20:03. https://www.ted.com/talks/brene_brown_the_power_of_vulnerability?language=en

Jeyachandran, Kishone. "The Beginners Mind (Shoshin)." Aug. 13, 2021. https://medium.com/@kishoreblog/the-beginners-mind-shoshin-c656c57b358e

Porter, Tony. "A Call to Men." TEDWomen. December 2010. 10:57. https://www.ted.com/talks/tony_porter_a_call_to_men

Chapter 6

Co-Active Training Institute. "Coactive Leadership Training." Accessed February 17, 2022. https://coactive.com/training/leadership-training/

Tiodar, Alexandra. "The Truth About Masculine and Feminine Energy Explained." November 15, 2021. https://subconsciousservant.com/masculine-and-feminine-energy/

Chapter 7

[none]

Chapter 8

American Foundation for Suicide Prevention. Retrieved, September 10, 2021. https://afsp.org/suicide-statistics

Davecrenshaw.com. "Home Page." Accessed January 22, 2022. https://davecrenshaw.com/

David, Susan. "Self-Compassion for the Self-Critical." May 4, 2020, in *Checking In with Susan David*. https://podcasts.apple.com/us/podcast/checking-in-with-susan-david/id1504596643

Gupta, T., and C. Hook. (2021). "Care Leads to Care: How Caring for Ourselves Helps Us Better Care for Others." Promundo-US. https://www.dove.com/us/en/men-care/paternity-leave/care-leads-to-care.html

Kaufman, Michael. "There's No Such Thing as a Real Man." The Telegraph. 2014. https://michaelkaufman.com/wp-content/uploads/2008/12/Kaufman-Theres-No-Such-Thing-as-a-Real-Man.pdf

McKoy, Jillian. "Depression Rates in US Tripled When the Pandemic First Hit—Now, They're Even Worse." Boston University School of Public Health. October 7, 2021. https://www.bu.edu/articles/2021/depression-rates-tripled-when-pandemic-first-hit/

Veal, Christopher. "The Vulnerable Man Episode 26—Jordan Holmes." July 19, 2021. In *The Vulnerable Man*. Produced by Christopher Veal. Podcast, MP3 audio, 45:36. https://vulnerableman.libsyn.com/vulnerable-man-ep026-jordan-holmes

Chapter 9

Manson, Mark. "Vulnerability: The Key to Better Relationships." https://markmanson.net/vulnerability-in-relationships

Sinek, Simon. "How Great Leaders Inspire Action." TEDx Puget Sound. September 2009. 17:48. https://www.ted.com/talks/simon_sinek_how_great_leaders_inspire_action?language=en

Chapter 10

Crossman, Matt. "Why You Need to Pace Yourself." SUCCESS Magazine. October 17, 2020. https://www.success.com/why-you-need-to-pace-yourself/

Veal, Christopher. "The Vulnerable Man Episode 36—Jim Young."
December 20, 2021. In *The Vulnerable Man*. Produced by
Christopher Veal. Podcast, MP3 audio, 49:46.
https://vulnerableman.libsyn.com/vulnerableman-ep036-jim-
young

Zamani Sani SH, Fathirezaie Z, Brand S, et al. "Physical activity
and self-esteem: testing direct and indirect relationships associated with psychological and physical mechanisms." *Neuro-
psychiatr Dis Treat.* 2016;12:2617-2625. Published Oct 12, 2016.
https://www.ncbi.nlm.nih.gov/pmc/articles/PMC5068479/

Chapter 11

Cuddy, Amy. Your Body Language May Shape Who You Are."
TEDGlobal 2012. June 2012. 20:46. https://www.ted.com/talks/
amy_cuddy_your_body_language_may_shape_who_you_are?
language=en

Logan, David. "Tribal Leadership." TEDx USC. March 2009. 16:22.
https://www.ted.com/talks/david_logan_tribal_leadership#
t-976361

Chapter 12

Clear, James. "Atomic Habits. An Easy & Proven Way to Build Good
Habits & Break Bad Ones." New York: Avery, 2018. (pg. 16)

Hirschi, Ivona. "Understanding 4 Stages of Adult Learning." Feb.
16, 2021. https://medium.com/top-hat/understand-4-stages-of-
adult-learning-build-new-skills-better-bafc2fd9b6f5